INTRODUCING
MICROCOMPUTERS
IN BUSINESS

TEACH YOURSELF BOOKS

INTRODUCING
MICROCOMPUTERS
IN BUSINESS

B. K. Pannell, D. C. Jackson
and S. B. Lucas

TEACH YOURSELF BOOKS

Hodder and Stoughton

First published by Enterprise Books as
Make A Success of Microcomputing in your Business
Copyright © 1981, 1983 Enterprise Books

Teach Yourself edition first published 1985
Copyright © 1985 Enterprise Books

British Library Cataloguing in Publication Data
Pannell, B. K.
Introducing microcomputers in business. – Teach
yourself ed. – (Teach yourself books)
1. Microcomputers
I. Title   II. Jackson, D. C. (David Cameron)
III. Lucas, S. B.   IV. Pannell, B. K. Make a
success of microcomputing in your business
V. Series
658′.022′0285404   HF5548.2

ISBN 0 340 37102 1

Printed and bound in Great Britain for
Hodder and Stoughton Educational,
a division of Hodder and Stoughton Ltd,
Mill Road, Dunton Green, Sevenoaks, Kent,
by Richard Clay (The Chaucer Press) Ltd,
Bungay, Suffolk. Photoset by
Rowland Phototypesetting Ltd,
Bury St Edmunds, Suffolk

Contents

Foreword

Since the invention of computers there has been a continual development of both hardware and software giving the users ever more cost effective solutions to their data processing problems. The recent advances in microelectronics, rightly called 'the micro revolution', have resulted in a dramatic fall in the price of computer hardware and it is now possible for even the smallest of businesses to consider the installation of a computer.

The difficulties for the first-time buyer of a small computer system are the wide variety of equipment available and the problem of understanding the jargon used in most computer literature. This book has been written for the owner or manager of a small business who is considering the possibility of computerising some of his business functions. No previous knowledge of computing has been assumed and the only technical aspects discussed in detail are those which could directly affect the success of the computer installation. The major part of the book is devoted to explaining a systematic approach to the task of computerisation. There are also several typical case studies which illustrate the approach.

A major problem when buying any new equipment is knowing the right questions to ask. I believe that the checklists will be of considerable value to the first-, or even the second-time buyer.

There are many books which describe the technical aspects of computing, but this is one of the few which is written for the businessman whose interest is solely to obtain successful use in his business. It may also appeal to those who advise small businesses regarding computer use. For its size it contains a large amount of useful information and I am very happy to recommend it to any businessman considering the potentially dangerous leap into computerisation.

Professor F. H. Sumner
*Barclays Professor of
Microprocessor Applications,
University of Manchester*

Preface

It is frequently stated that computer installations seldom meet expectations, but despite this criticism many small installations are being ordered every day. Expectations are perhaps unduly high; successful installation is certainly less common than it should be.

A reason for unduly high expectation is the continued existence of a number of myths, particularly in regard to the use of computers for business. A few examples will suffice to make the point:

'A computer gives a fresh start and overcomes business weakness.'
It does not. Faults of business organisation and method, unless clearly recognised and corrected, will be perpetuated and made worse by installing a computer.

'Computing is done at school by my twelve year old – so there can be no problem for adults to use one in my business.'
This statement ignores the major differences between computing in school and computing in business, which is concerned with processing large volumes of data and the provision of management information.

'A computer can be bought for under £100, so I should get a suitable system for my business very cheaply.'
This again confuses the requirements of a school pupil or hobbyist with those of business. The printer for a small business installation for instance can cost more than the computing unit.

'A recommendation from a friend as to a good type of computer is all I need.'
It is not. Well written programs, carefully selected and adapted for each business, are the first requisite. The computer hardware is a secondary question.

This book came to be written partly to explode these myths and partly to lead the small businessman through what is now the bewildering jungle of computer specialisms.

For the small businessman the problems of installing a computer are in many ways similar to those faced by the large business. He needs to analyse his business requirements and he needs to choose programs which reflect those requirements. But the cash which can be afforded for these necessary tasks will be far less than that available to large businesses. Thus the small businessman is in a dilemma and he has little choice but to take some risks. How to minimise those risks and how to move step by step towards sensible decisions is the principal purpose of this book.

1

Introducing Success

Development of the small business computer

Prior to 1955 computer development was largely confined to a few universities in Britain and America. The main uses for the machines were seen to lie in the rapid solution of well-defined mathematical and scientific problems. This stream of development continued, but in addition the mid-1950s saw the first practical attempts to use computers for government administration and business purposes, followed by twenty years of very rapid development in both streams of activity. On the one hand computers were designed to undertake more complex scientific calculations at faster speeds. On the other, there was an increasing demand for storage devices (magnetic tapes and disks) and for fast printers to handle the high volume of data involved in government and large business applications. Typical of this period was the large computer, referred to normally today as a 'mainframe'.

The advent of minicomputers in the mid-1960s made little impact on the mainframe market. The minicomputer was designed primarily for mathematical and engineering applications, with an emphasis on ease of use by the individual mathematician, scientist or engineer. The individual keyed in his program* or data (by using a keyboard similar to a typewriter) and obtained printed results by

---

*A program is simply a list of very detailed instructions for carrying out a particular job. A program package is a small group of related programs, suitable for carrying out a specific job, e.g. payroll. The terms are explained in Chapter 3.

use of a teleprinter. Ease of use was obtained partly by this direct interplay between the individual operator and his machine and partly by improved computer 'languages' for writing programs.

The modern business computer has been developed from both mainframe and minicomputer design experience. From mainframe it derives the systems for effective computer use in business problems, including methods for the storage and printing of substantial volumes of data. From minicomputers it derives ease of use, and in addition much of the basic technology helped contribute to its low cost.

Reasons for growth since the mid-1970s

Since the mid-1970s the demand for small business computers has grown rapidly. The main reasons for this growth are:

1 The development of suitable computing equipment and simplified methods of computer use;
2 Falling costs of equipment. Equipment suitable for a limited range of business functions can be obtained for £1,000 (at 1984 prices). A system for more general use in a small business would typically cost from £5,000;
3 The growth in generalised programs which can, within limits, be adapted to meet the requirements of individual businesses. Use of these program packages avoids the high costs of writing programs for each new user;
4 The increasing cost of clerical labour.

How a computer can help a small business

The general conception of a computer is that it is a machine which can operate very quickly. Correctly programmed for any particular task, and given all the data it needs for that task, a computer can produce results far more rapidly than a clerk. Thus there is potential for staff savings. In a small business, however, every clerk normally has a great variety of tasks to perform and when due allowance has been made for the clerical effort involved in getting data into the computer and for the time taken to complete other associated functions, staff savings in a small business may be small. Typically, rather than a direct reduction in the numbers employed, the installation of a computer is likely to provide scope for business expansion without the need for extra staff. It will also provide for much more effective use of staff when it replaces accounting machines and other similar electro-mechanical equipment.

Another way in which a computer can assist small business is in the provision of information for immediate operational use. For example, there are systems in use which, following a telephone or personal enquiry, will at once display the availability of a stock item. Similarly, computer systems for hotels have been developed to show immediately the rooms available for reservation. In this type of work the use of computers is particularly valuable when the information is required at more than one station or when changes have to be recorded at one or more points (e.g. shop floor) but the resulting information is required elsewhere (e.g. sales office or accounting section). The essential advantage in such situations is that the computer is acting as a centralised record which has up-to-the-minute information irrespective of where the changes occur or of where the information is required.

The main advantage is the one which is most generally claimed for the small business. It is the collection of information which is important in business management and control. This normally means accounting information. Even quite small businesses have problems with credit and stock control, in analysing which are their more and less profitable lines and in rapidly and frequently assessing their trading position to guide their future activity. The small computer can without question make major improvements in all these areas. Moreover, once suitable systems for basic accounting functions have been developed, little extra effort is required to analyse the data which has been put into these systems to provide further control information. For example, it is easy to compare gross sales or sales by product or area with budgeted sales, or with the sales for previous years.

These various advantages which are undoubtedly obtainable from computer use are, however, frequently not achieved. Although much has been done to simplify computing methods, effective computer use in business depends on recognition of the problems involved in that particular business. Despite common elements in the business use of computers no business is quite like any other business when examined at the level of detail appropriate for computer system design. An appreciation of these differences is a necessary preliminary to understanding what makes for successful computer use.

Variety of business situations

Businesses can be classified in many different ways. Three broad classifications are *manufacturing*, *distributive* and *service*, but within each of these there are possibly hundreds of different trades. Within each trade there can be differences in the sizes of business, in the number of sites used, and in production methods. Also wide variations in the precise services offered to customers, differences in stocking and sales policies and in product pricing methods. In addition there will be varying styles of management approach – that is to say in any given situation one manager will see a need for particular information which could differ substantially from a view taken by another manager. Finally there is the important question of the *volume* of data to be stored in the computer. Businesses vary significantly in the number of suppliers and customers, the number of accounts handled, the number of stock lines and in many other ways which are significant in the final choice of a computing system.

To meet this bewildering variety of business situations there stands the computer, a machine which will do precisely what it is instructed to do – neither more nor less. Its instructions are carried in its programs. The key problem is, of course, to write or purchase programs which are suited to the requirements of the particular business. But the requirements are never self-evident. It is not good enough to say that our firm is very much the same as Smith Ltd on the other side of town and if computer X works there it will work here. Such comparisons are valuable but insufficient and, unless the differences are also seen, will be misleading. Before programs can be written or chosen, there is a need to specify requirements both in the broad terms of business intention and organisation and in the more detailed sense of the volume of data required and methods of application.

'We mustn't feed those questions to the computer. We require answers
that are evasive and ambiguous – I'll deal with them.'

(*Punch*)

Key factors for success

The classical approach to the problem of specifying requirements
which has been followed by large companies, usually using mainframe computers, has been a very detailed specification of requirements drawn up by professional systems analysts working in con-
junction with managers. Many man-years have been required for
these studies and the costs involved have been high – so high indeed
that for small business they would normally be prohibitive. The
problem has been reduced by the introduction of generalised
programs, in other words software packages. Nonetheless, for the
small business there is really no alternative but that the owner or
one of the directors should personally outline the requirements and
to some extent fill in the detail before considering a purchase. How
best 'to make use of consultants or suppliers is one of the main
concerns of this book. It has, however, to be recognised that lack of

a full specification implies risk of part or total failure. It is a risk which based purely on cost grounds may have to be taken, but one which should be minimised in every possible way.

For the successful installation of a business computer there are essentially three prerequisites:

1   That the directors or owner(s) of the business should be committed to a methodical approach to the problems involved and that one of them should be able to devote considerable time to system definition, negotiations with suppliers and supervision of systems implementation;
2   That the work to be done should be adequately defined;
3   That the full cost should be assessed and recognised.

The first point is of such importance that it is developed immediately below. The problem of definition is described in detail in Chapter 8 and costs described in Appendix A.

Commitment by directors/owners to the project may seem an obvious requirement, but in the day-to-day concerns of sales and production, many owners have not the time to stand back from their immediate problems to take the long term view required for computer installation. Again the problems of definition may not be recognised or the whole project may be dismissed as if the computer were little more than a typewriter. Allied to these views the directors may consider that for a capital sum of say £10,000 they are buying a system and it is the supplier's job to ensure that the computer meets the requirements of the business. The supplier will at least nominally agree with this point of view but his profit margins will generally be insufficient to permit more than a quick overview of requirements. The client who is not really clear as to his needs and who does not insist on them is hardly in a position to complain if the system fails to do what in hindsight he feels it ought to do. There is, of course, a temptation after the event to impute all the blame to the supplier but this is seldom fully justified and in any event it is the user that is most likely to suffer.

The importance of director/owner commitment to a computer installation cannot be overstressed. Successful computer installation demands time and study and the basic reason for complete or partial failure in a small business is likely to be an absence of this involvement. It is possible, of course, that a director or owner may be inhibited from taking an active part in the installation of a computer because, while vaguely recognising the need, he feels he has insufficient technical knowledge. However, a lack of technical knowledge about the way a computer works is not altogether a handicap. It is far more important to see the wood than the trees and the wood in this context consists of an appreciation of the business requirement, a balanced assessment of the advantages of computer use and a wise choice of supplier. A short course in programming (say five evenings) would help to develop an understanding of what computer use involves, but a knowledge of programming is by no means essential for the businessman.

It must also be recognised that even after a computer is installed there will be a need for continuing commitment by the owner/ director of the company. Business conditions seldom remain static and experience in the use of the computer almost always results in demands for further changes. It is essential that the owner/director ensures that these changes occur in a manner and at a rate that is tolerable to the business. This question is examined in Chapter 10.

It is important that the owner of the business remains in overall control of the process of computerisation. The responsibility for this cannot be delegated to computer consultants or suppliers.

Bureau service as an alternative to computer installation

If the owner or director cannot devote the necessary time to the work involved in installing a computer, use of a bureau service may provide a suitable answer. There is still, of course, a need to decide what work is to be done by computer and to reach a clear agreement with the bureau as to what is expected of the bureau and what the bureau expects of its client, for example, relating to the submission of data to be fed into the computer. On the other hand most of the problems of installing and running a computer are carried by the bureau and the client's commitment as such is minimal. As a bonus the experience gained in using a bureau is likely to be valuable in subsequently assessing the merits of the in-house computer.

Bureau services are explained in Chapter 2. Although the user of bureau services may find much of interest in the remainder of this book, it is written primarily for the benefit of those who wish to install or expand in-house computing.

2

Computer Bureaux

A bureau has much to offer the first-time user who does not want to devote the management time needed to develop a satisfactory in-house system or who has very specialised requirements for which program packages are not otherwise available. Costs compared with in-house computing will sometimes be high but where the volumes of input or output are small, the cost advantages may be with the bureau. Moreover, if the work required can await a period in the week when computing work is scarce, the bureau may offer exceptionally low rates.

Services provided by computer bureaux fall into two main categories: *batch* and *time-sharing*.

Batch services

The batch service is so called because it typically accepts a batch of input documents from one or more clients, processes them and sends back printed outputs to the client. Many hundreds of payrolls are processed in this way. The method is also popular for the preparation of mailing lists, membership records and for some accounting systems.

In the simplest form of batch service, the bureau undertakes data preparation, in other words the keying (entering data by keyboard) of data from the client's documents in order that it can be input to the computer. Such a service has benefits and disadvantages when compared with the use of an in-house computer.

The benefits:
1 Very little computer knowledge is required by the client;
2 The client has no capital investment in computing, requires little or no special training, and has no special responsibility for the work except to see that the end result meets his requirements.

There are also disadvantages:
1 Time is inevitably lost in transmitting documents, in the various batch activities of the bureau (data preparation, computing, output control) and in returning printed outputs;
2 The client cannot control priorities for urgent work; he must expect that his work will be done at agreed times, and occasionally delayed;
3 Costs may be high when compared with the use of a small in-house computer. In making a comparison, however, care should be taken to ensure that all elements of costs for the in-house installation are taken into account (see Appendix A).

There are variations on this basic form of batch service which are becoming increasingly popular. In one such variation, the client keys his data into some form of terminal device and data is transferred by telephone line to the bureau. This reduces the turnround time involved and allows the client to retain input documents. A further reduction of turnround time can be achieved when the client has a terminal which can also produce the printed outputs. Such terminals, however, can be more costly than small in-house computers.

Time-sharing services

Time-sharing services offered by the bureaux are aimed for the most part at providing a computing service to an individual manager, engineer or accountant or to a group of people who may share the use of a terminal. Terminals have keyboards for input and either typewriters or screens for output. A number of clients may be linked to the bureau computer through such terminals but the terminals are slow in operation while the computer is generally large and very fast. Thus many users may be simultaneously served by the computer and no one user will be aware of use by another. The computer's time is shared by all and gives an apparently instantaneous service to each. From the user's point of view there is no problem of scheduling work. His terminal is able to gain access to the computer at any time.

The user of a time-sharing service may either develop his own programs from his terminal or use packages provided by the bureau. The availability of highly specialised packages, typically for engineering calculations and business planning which may not otherwise be obtainable, is an important element in selling time-sharing services and a small business, for example a consultancy requiring the use of such specialist programs, could sensibly consider time-sharing. Use of time-sharing for bulk repetitive work is, however, likely to be uneconomic.

Selection of a bureau

A list of computer bureaux can readily be compiled by reference to the telephone and computer directories, and publications such as the Computer Users' Year Book. In drawing up a shortlist of possible bureaux, regard should be paid to the points listed below:

1 **Location**   Close proximity is particularly valuable for batch services, for it reduces both transport time and cost. It also makes it easier for bureau support staff and client to meet, and when communication is largely by telephone it reduces line costs;

2 **Bureau expertise**   No bureau can have staff who are expert in all computing applications and some have not the programming staff to adapt standard packages to a client's particular requirements. Enquiries, preferably through existing users of a bureau, may establish where its experience lies;

3 **Costs**   These could vary significantly between one bureau and another because of experience in the chosen field and the possible availability of marginal or free time.

If the work at the bureau is seen as a forerunner to an in-house installation, it should not be assumed that the bureau programs will necessarily run on a suitable in-house machine. It is likely to be difficult to find a small machine which will be compatible even if the programs could be transferred, and the bureau contract may not allow a transfer.

No particular difficulty should arise in agreeing contractual arrangements with a bureau. If, however, the bureau fixes a minimum period for the contract or has to make an initial charge for set up or program writing, greater care will obviously be needed to ensure that value for money is obtained.

Terminals are normally hired from the bureau but if purchase is required then it is desirable to ensure that the terminal will be compatible with other bureau services which the client may possibly wish to use.

One practical problem is the assessment of the charges which a bureau will make. Charges are normally based in whole or in part on 'computing units' but although these may be well understood by the bureau, their definition will probably be anything but simple to the user. The user has really no choice but to ask for specimen charges based on a trial run(s). Another difficult point where errors occur in the print out is the charging and invoicing for re-runs according to whether the error is deemed to be the fault of the user or the bureau.

3

Microcomputer Software

Software is the name given to the assembly of instructions which control the computer and enable it to do useful work.

Before considering the individual components of a microcomputer system it is worth making a general comparison between a human or manual system and a computer equivalent. Let us imagine an intending book-keeper arriving for his first day's work. We will assume he has received a general education at school, but has no previous experience of book-keeping. He will therefore have the ability to read and understand written instructions and to do arithmetic. With this amount of knowledge he is not going to be immediately useful as a book-keeper because he has no knowledge of the steps required to perform such a task. In this state he is roughly equivalent to a microcomputer which has just been switched on.

The microcomputer will have the ability to do arithmetic and will also be able to 'understand' certain instructions (given in the correct language) but would be unable to perform a task such as up-dating a sales ledger.

In order for the book-keeper to be able to perform a useful task he has either to be shown what to do or be given a set of written instructions which are sufficiently detailed and precise that, using only his current knowledge and ability, he is able to follow the instructions and carry out the task. In a manual system such a set of instructions could well be a textbook. For a computer the set of instructions will be the application program.

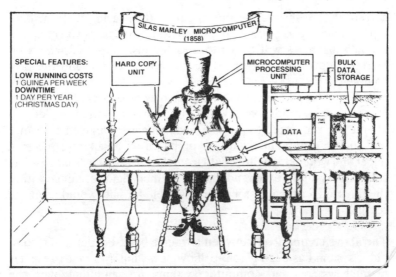

Let us imagine that the textbook and the computer program equivalent contain instructions for the maintenance of a sales ledger. The first instruction in the textbook will probably tell the trainee to ask if there are invoices awaiting processing. If so, he will be told to look at the first invoice and to identify the customer's name and address. Having done this he will then be instructed to open the sales ledger and to locate the entries relating to this particular customer. The computer system will do exactly the same.

The program will cause the computer to enquire (via the visual display unit or screen) whether there is data to be processed. If there is, the details of the invoice will have to be typed into the computer via the keyboard. Having entered the customer's name and address the program will cause the computer to search its own ledger/filing system, the disk files, until it locates the file corresponding to the customer in question.

The next step in the process will require the trainee to up-date the ledger. His textbook will tell him exactly how to do this and he will need to make use of his mathematical ability to create the new balance in the ledger. Having done this calculation he will make the entry in the ledger and ask for the next invoice, or if there are no more invoices he will close the ledger as the task is complete. The computer system, having located the customer's file, will read the current data from the file into memory then, using the new data typed in via the keyboard, the calculations will be performed and the new balances will be written to the disk files. If there is no further data to be processed the file will be closed and the task complete.

The final function which the trainee may be expected to perform is to produce a report based on the information in the sales ledger. He may be requested to prepare a statement for a given customer and such a statement would be prepared on a separate piece of paper and would use figures/data from the sales ledger. Likewise the computer system would read into the memory data contained within the sales ledger file and then, in a suitable format, would print the report.

The above comparison between a trainee book-keeper and a computer system has been given to show how similar in many respects manual systems and computer systems are, and that even the component parts of each system have equivalents. There are, of course, differences of which it is necessary to be aware. There are obvious variations in speed and accuracy. A computer system will in general be very much faster than a manual system and much more accurate. On the other hand, the trainee book-keeper will eventually learn the instructions in his textbook and will soon be able to dispense with the textbook altogether. The computer will never do this and each time the system is switched off, program information is lost and must be re-loaded again next time. Perhaps even more important, after some experience, the trainee will be able to make educated guesses at pieces of information (instructions or data) which are unclear for some reason. Maybe a name has been mis-spelt, the data is obviously incorrect, or something just 'looks wrong'. The computer will require information to be entered correctly and accurately, and whilst some data checking can be built into programs, it is generally true that greater accuracy is required for data entry in a computer system.

It should be apparent from the above discussion that, no matter how intelligent the trainee, he will be unable to perform useful book-keeping tasks until he is given a set of instructions. The computer system is exactly the same and, however powerful the microprocessor or however large and fast the disk store, until the

computer is loaded with a program to perform a given task it is useless. Therefore it is strongly recommended that when considering a computer system for a small business the prospective purchaser should start his evaluation not with the computer itself, but with the program to perform his required task.

Software can be considered under three separate headings:

1 programming languages;
2 application software;
3 system software.

Programming languages

The computer itself is only able to understand instructions which are in *binary* or *machine code* (a series of 0's or 1's). However, this code is difficult for humans to work with, since in order to program a computer efficiently it is necessary for the programmer to remember the commonly used codes. Programming would be an incredibly tiresome task if it were necessary to refer to a code book for every single instruction. Humans are not very good at recognising or remembering codes composed of patterns of 0's and 1's and it is necessary therefore to find a means of overcoming this problem. The most common means is the use of a 'high-level' language.

A high-level language provides the programmer with statements or commands which are written in English or mathematical formats, thus providing very much easier programming, particularly in data processing applications. However, the computer can only execute machine code instructions and it is therefore necessary to provide a translation program which will convert the high-level language statements to machine code. These translation programs are known as compilers or interpreters depending on whether the whole program is translated into machine language before running the program or the program is translated a line at a time during execution. For the business user, the practical difference between the two is that the computer will run some programs very much faster after using a compiler than when the interpreter is used.

Selection of a high-level language for a microcomputer has until recently been largely a question of taking what was available with the particular machine purchased. This was in most cases BASIC. BASIC is a language which was developed for teaching purposes and is particularly easy to learn (at least as far as the programming of simple tasks). However, it does have a number of disadvantages, being particularly slow in execution in the interpreted form. Each manufacturer has also tended to implement a *dialect* of BASIC peculiar to his machine, which has made it difficult to transfer programs from one computer to another. Nevertheless, it is a widely used language and a very high proportion of programs for business application are written in BASIC.

Other languages are now becoming available, and in particular COBOL and Pascal can be used on most microcomputers and can have a number of advantages over BASIC.

Application software

Application software is written to perform a specific task or process such as accounting, payroll, mailing lists, and so on, and the majority of application software is written in a high-level language.

For the prospective first-time computer purchaser the application software is the most important aspect to consider, following the initial definition of the problem and the fundamental requirements as detailed in Chapter 1.

Assuming that the task to be carried out has been correctly

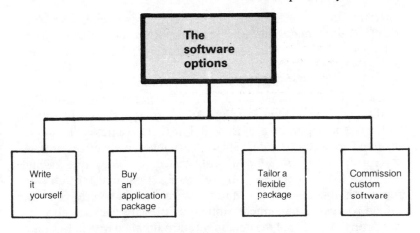

Figure 1

identified and carefully defined, the prospective user is faced with essentially four alternative sources for his application software, as shown in Figure 1.

Normal and super high-level software packages

Software packages refer to a set of computer programs which have been written to perform a specific, commonly required task. Each program is written in such a way that it is applicable to a large number of companies, in other words it is intended for a large market. This has the advantage that the package will be relatively cheap, since the cost of the software is spread over a number of users. The major disadvantage of the general purpose software package is that it is unlikely to fulfil all the requirements of prospective users and thus some compromise may have to be made by the purchaser. It is possible to tailor some packages to accommodate specific requirements of prospective users, but this would normally have to be done by the original supplier and may add to the cost. It is extremely difficult to modify, except in a trivial way, programs written by someone else.

Packages exist for most of the standard accounting/book-keeping tasks required by the small business. This can result in rapid implementation which is an important point in favour of packaged software, as custom software or self-written programs are notoriously slow in materialising. However, there are further disadvantages associated with packaged software. Probably the most important disadvantage will relate to program errors. It is frequently not realised by people new to computing that computer programs often have inherent errors, and that such errors will often be difficult to detect and correct. A well tried and tested package will have the major 'bugs' removed, but there is a possibility of undetected errors lurking in rarely used branches of the program. This sort of error can, in general, only be corrected by the original writer of the program. It is therefore essential that the software supplier is able to provide genuine program maintenance.

The successful implementation of a software package also depends on the quality of the documentation supplied with it, since it is common for the purchaser to implement the package with little outside help. A well written package from a professional software source will come with properly produced manuals, which will thoroughly explain how the package works and will provide information on how to overcome the majority of accidental errors or malfunctions. A program package supplied with a couple of typed A4 sheets, stapled together, should be immediately rejected. The program has probably been written in exactly the same style as the 'manual'.

A point for consideration with packaged software is that future integration of separate business functions may be difficult or even impossible. For example, following successful implementation of a stock control package it might be considered advantageous to implement an order handling system. There would obviously be considerable advantages to be gained from linking these two functions. Receipt of an order would automatically cause current stock levels to be checked and record stock to be allocated to the customer. This type of linking is virtually impossible if the separate functions are performed by individual unrelated packages. This need is met by some software houses who provide integrated sets of programs which may be bought and implemented one at a time, and allow full cross-communication between programs.

Custom software

The term *custom software* refers to computer programs which have been professionally written to match the user's requirements exactly. The obvious advantage is that, being written to match needs, implementation should involve a minimum of reorganisation of business procedures. If written by a professional software source, the programs should be of high quality, well tested, well documented and the supplier should be able to provide a first class maintenance service. Future integration of separate functions should be straightforward, providing the supplier was made aware of this possibility when first contacted to provide the programs.

The most important disadvantage of this approach will be its cost. The writing of computer programs is highly labour intensive, requiring skilled individuals who command good salaries. Since the program is being prepared as a 'one-off', the full cost of preparation will be reflected in the price. Thus, whilst a packaged order processing program for a microcomputer is unlikely to cost more than £1,000, a custom program could easily cost between £5,000 and £10,000. The prospective first-time computer user is strongly recommended to consider commissioning custom software only if he is absolutely certain that a program package which will meet a substantial proportion of his requirement does not exist.

Write it yourself

The program written by the user can be the most satisfactory solution. This is because it will have been written by someone who understands exactly what is required of the final product. It will be an exact match to the needs of the business, faults can be corrected and future modifications swiftly implemented. The program can grow with the business.

However, there is one great disadvantage. Computer programming is not easy – at least not at the professional level required for programs on which the future of the business may depend. It is perfectly true that a week-end course on programming in the language BASIC can enable one to write programs to check income tax or to keep the bank balance up to date. But programs of this type are vastly different from the program that will enable processing of

'Oh, that charge is for computerising the bill.'

(*Punch*)

large amounts of data, maintain files and quickly retrieve required items of information. Programming can be done by the businessman and people have made a success of it. However, the magnitude of the task should not be under-estimated.

Time requirements that apply to the professional programmer apply equally to the businessman with an aptitude to program. It is vital not to overlook the need for thoroughness in initial design, debugging and documentation. The program author cannot be present one hundred per cent of the time and staff will have to use the computer in his absence, so they will need instructions and manuals to which they can refer.

Super high-level language packages

Programming in conventional high-level languages such as COBOL, FORTRAN, Pascal and BASIC requires a reasonable knowledge of what is going on inside the computer. While it is not necessary (albeit helpful) to know how the computer interprets pulses of electricity as instructions or data, it is necessary to know how the computer files information, the limitations as to the type of data it can handle and the instructions it can execute. It is also necessary to be able to break down a complex manual task into a series of simpler tasks which can be handled by the computer.

However, since 1981 there has been a major growth in packages for microcomputers which enable the user to 'program' the computer in a much simpler manner, requiring very little detailed knowledge of what is actually going on inside. These 'super high-level language' packages require the user to set up a model for his particular business function, but the instructions are simple and generally closely related to the way in which a manual system would be set up.

One of the most widely used packages in this category is the program VisiCalc (the trade mark of Personal Software Inc.). This program provides the user with a large 'electronic sheet' which is ideal for performing cash flow forecasts or estimates. It can also be used for keeping incomplete records or as a day book for a business where the number of transactions is fairly low. With little more than a few hours' experience, it is possible to design quite sophisticated financial models which can be stored on a disk and re-used or modified as required. Other popular packages of the spread sheet type are Supercalc and Multiplan, and a spread sheet program is now available for any popular make of microcomputer. Typical applications will most commonly involve some form of costing, but some spread sheets now have sorting facilities which open up new possibilities such as sales performance analysis.

Another example of this type of package is a database management system. This is essentially a sophisticated filing cabinet in which the user defines by means of simple instructions how the items (fields) within each record are set up. The computer will then allow certain sophisticated procedures to be carried out on the records.

For example, a database system may be used for maintaining customer records for a travel agency. The fields within each record might contain information such as customer name, address, destination, tour operator, departure date, duration, total cost, and so on. The database system would allow the identification of all customers whose records met certain criteria selected by the person using the computer. Thus it would be simple to identify all customers living in City A who took holidays in the Bahamas in January 1981 with tour operator XYZ.

In general a database system can provide the user with a list of data from within the data base file, sorted by any of the fields. Furthermore, sub-lists may be obtained by the use of acceptance criteria such as 'less than', 'more than' or 'equal'. Some database packages available for micros can correlate information from more than one file, but facilities to do this are limited and care is needed in their selection.

The advantages of super high-level language packages are that little computing knowledge is required, they are generally inexpensive and they are flexible in the range of applications for which they can be used. The disadvantages are that they will not be quite as simple to use as a standard application package, particularly where there are relatively high volumes of routine input data. It is envisaged that database systems (or information retrieval systems) will be a major growth area in microcomputing.

System software

The terms *system software* or *operating system* refer to the program instructions which enable the computer to interact with external devices or peripherals such as printers and disk drives, and which controls the organisation of application programs and data. The system software is normally provided by the supplier of the computer hardware and for most purposes it is not something that the first-time computer user need be too concerned about.

However, there is one aspect of system software which is worth considering when assessing computer systems and that is the software that enables disk file access, commonly known as the disk operating system or DOS. One of the most irritating features of small computer systems has been that application programs have not been portable, i.e. they cannot be readily transferred from one machine to another. To a certain extent this has been due to different dialects of BASIC being supplied by different manufacturers. However the most important hindrance to portability has been the totally different disk operating system software. This has meant that disk files written by, say, a PET computer, could not be read by an Apple. However, there are a small number of operating systems which allow portability of programs between different computers. Probably the most widely known example is CP/M (registered trade mark of Digital Research) but other operating systems such as IBM's PC-DOS and UNIX offer similar portability and standardisation.

4

Microcomputer
Hardware

Hardware is the name given to the physical parts of a microcomputer

The computer system consists of the central processor (CPU) together with read only memory (ROM) and random access memory (RAM), plus keyboard, video monitor, disk drives and a printer. The central processor, read only memory and random access memory are housed together in a single cabinet, while the video monitor, disk drives and keyboard may be included in the one cabinet or may be plug-in peripherals. In most cases the printer will be a plug-in peripheral.

The function of the individual components are detailed below:

Central Processing Unit (CPU) This component, commonly known as the 'microprocessor' or 'central processor', performs the task of organising the work of all the other components and also carries out arithmetic, sorting and similar functions.

Read Only Memory (ROM) This component contains certain program instructions which are required by the central processor for its own internal use and do not change. The BASIC language interpreter is frequently held in the read only memory, the function of the interpreter being to transform the program instructions in the 'English-like' language BASIC into instructions which the central processor can directly carry out.

Random Access Memory (RAM) This is the computer's workspace in which the application program instructions will reside together with the data currently being worked on. It is important to remember that the central processor can only manipulate data or execute application program instructions which are currently held in random access memory. In most computer systems, program instructions and data stored in random memory are lost when the computer is switched off.

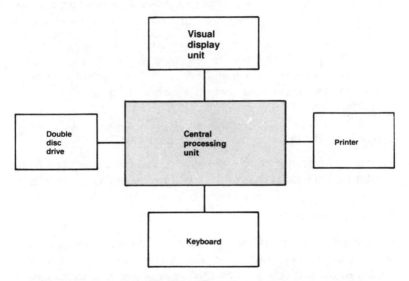

Figure 2 A block diagram of a typical microcomputer system which might be suitable for a small business.

Visual Display Unit (VDU) When the video monitor and keyboard are contained in a separate unit, this unit is termed a visual display unit (VDU). The unit provides the means by which the computer communicates rapidly with the user. Thus, when it is necessary for the user to enter data a suitable prompt will appear on the video screen and the computer will wait until the data has been entered.

Keyboard The means by which new data or instructions can be entered into the computer, by simply 'typing-in' the information.

Disk Drive(s) The disk drive provides a means for permanent storage (on a magnetically coated disk) of both programs and data, with the facility for rapid access and re-entry of information. The disk drive provides the capacity to store or file information which would otherwise be lost when the computer is switched off. The time taken to locate a specific item of data is typically about 0.1 sec. for a floppy disk drive or 0.0001–0.01 sec. for a hard disk drive.

Audio Cassette Drive The cassette drive is another means of providing permanent storage of programs and data and is substantially cheaper than a disk system. It is, however, not in common use in business computer systems as it suffers from the disadvantage of being extremely slow in operation; for example, an item of data stored at one end of a C60 audio cassette would require a 30 minute search before being located.

Printer The printer enables a paper record to be produced from information which is currently stored in random access memory.

Processor capacity

It is not proposed in this book to discuss the differing capabilities of the various microcomputer hardware systems on the market. The quality of the software is of overriding importance when assessing and choosing a microcomputer system, and selection of suitable software will in many cases define the hardware components required. Nevertheless, there are certain aspects of capacity of which the intending purchaser should be aware and these will be briefly discussed.

Many advertisements for microcomputer systems go into some detail about the power and speed of the chosen microprocessor chip. This information need not concern the average small business user. What matters is the speed with which the computer can process his particular workload. This is based on many factors and perhaps the most important is the skill with which the software has been written. For example, a competent programmer will write critical sections of the program in machine language in order to increase the speed of execution by a factor of 10 to 100 times the rate of corresponding operations carried out in interpreted BASIC.

In terms of the computer itself, an important aspect of capacity is the amount of random access memory available after the operating system and interpreter have been loaded. Memory size is measured in bytes, where one byte typically holds one character. Most early microcomputers were limited to a maximum of 65,536 bytes of random access memory (normally abbreviated to 64K, where 1K equals 1,024 bytes), but new generation microcomputers may have several megabytes of random excess memory.

It is important to remember that not only does the application program reside in random memory, but that all the data to be processed must be present at some time in random access memory. In order therefore to process large amounts of data efficiently and/or execute complex programs it is desirable to have as much random access memory available as possible. Many of the early microcomputer systems were produced with only 8K, or even 4K of random access memory which for general business application is insufficient. A business computer configuration should have at least 64K of available random access memory.

The 16-bit microcomputer

Up to 1982 most microcomputers had been based upon 8-bit microprocessors. That is, the basic unit for manipulating computer information within the microprocessor consists of 8 binary digits. There is now available a new generation of low cost microcomputers based upon 16-bit microprocessors. The advantage of systems based upon the 16-bit microprocessors is that they can manipulate information much more rapidly than corresponding 8-bit systems and they can be provided with much larger directly addressable random access memories (up to several megabytes).

Whilst there are many factors that govern the choice of a computer system, such as software and service, all other things being equal the 16-bit microcomputer is preferable to the 8-bit machine.

Disk storage capacity

The aspect of capacity of great concern to the business user is how much information can be stored on the disk drives. The reason for this is that in most business applications it is necessary to keep on file a record of every transaction or entry. A computerised accounting system which does not produce an audit trail is useless. It is all very well knowing that the current balance of an account is X, but it is absolutely essential to be able to trace back, entry by entry, how that balance came about. All this information will have to be kept on a disk file. The method of calculating the anticipated storage requirements for a particular application is something which any reputable supplier should be able to help the prospective purchaser determine.

There are, of course, financial implications involved, and not surprisingly, additional storage capacity incurs additional cost. The cheapest available disk systems are 5¼-inch drives which will provide approximately 100 to 200K characters of storage per floppy disk. These drives will vary in cost from about £150 to £250 each, including the necessary control electronics. It is, however, generally a requirement that a business system should have at least two disk drives. The reason being that it is important for security and protection against accidental damage. Copies of important data held on disks should be made regularly. It is possible to copy data files using only one disk drive, but it is a laborious procedure and the only sensible method is to use two drives and copy directly from one to the other. An additional advantage of having two or more drives is that many programs can be run using only one drive and therefore should a disk drive failure occur it is still possible to continue in operation.

The density at which information is being stored on floppy disks is steadily increasing and for a slightly higher expenditure, of about £500 per drive, it is possible to obtain storage capacities of between 400K and 600K per 5¼-inch floppy disk. Double-sided disk drives of this type can provide over one megabyte of storage per 5¼-inch disk. It is possible to split files so that, for example, a mailing list which requires 200K of file storage could be stored with half the list on a single floppy disk of 100K capacity and the other half of the list on the second floppy disk. However, this practice can become very tedious if large amounts of data are being processed as it will be necessary to continually exchange disks.

If 5¼-inch floppy disks offer insufficient storage capacity the next option is to consider the 8-inch size. These will give storage capacities of between 1 and 2 million (mega) bytes per floppy disk and will cost between £600 and £1,200 for a pair.

The third option for disk storage is to use hard disks. Hard disks are now becoming more readily available for microcomputers, costing from £1,000 upwards. Hard disks have storage capacities ranging from 3 megabytes to 64 megabytes per drive and access time 10 to 100 times faster than floppy disk drives.

A conservative rule of thumb concerning disk drive capacity is to purchase twice the capacity required for normal day-to-day running.

VDU screen size

Little needs to be said about the VDU or display monitor except that it should display at least 80 characters per line. Many of the cheaper microcomputers provide only a 40 character per line display. This is not really acceptable for business use because a typed sheet of A4 will normally contain 60 to 80 characters per line. It is vital when using a computer system for word processing to be able to see on the screen exactly what will be printed on paper. In addition, an 80 character screen will be able to display twice as much information as a 40 character screen, which can speed up many tasks.

Printer quality and speed

The choice of printer will be largely governed by the type of application and the quality of print required. From the above discussion on the VDU it should be apparent that the printer must also be capable of 80 characters per line, and for many applications 132 characters per line may be desirable.

Many printers can be switched from 80 characters to 132 characters per line either manually or under program control. The quality of print will be governed by the mechanism used to produce the printed characters. The cheaper printers employ a print head which contains a number of pins and each pin produces a dot on the paper. Printing of characters is effected by selecting appropriate pins to compose the desired character from a series of dots. The pins are arranged in a matrix usually ranging from 7 pins by 5 pins to 9 pins by 9 pins. In general, the more pins in the matrix the better the print quality.

The quality of print obtained has improved considerably recently, but the characters will always be composed of dots and as such are not of the same quality as the type-written page. The alternative is to use a daisy wheel printer in which the individual characters are held on the ends of a spiked plastic wheel, rather like the petals of a daisy. The wheel can be made to rotate in order to select the desired character, which strikes the ribbon, in much the same way as a conventional typewriter and the quality of the print obtained is therefore comparable with an electric typewriter. Typical costs for a dot matrix printer start from about £200, whereas a daisy wheel printer will cost between £700 and £2,000.

The speed of the printer may be of considerable importance in some businesses, while in others it will be relatively unimportant. The deciding factor will be the number, length and frequency of printed reports required. If the applications demand long print-outs then a high speed printer can produce a considerable saving in time. The best method of making a judgment is to find a user with a similar application to the one being considered and to enquire whether the printer speed is causing bottlenecks in the processing of data.

The upgrade path

It is necessary when purchasing hardware to consider that use of the computer will probably increase and that the original equipment may prove to be inadequate to perform all the tasks required.

There are three ways in which this problem of computer capacity may be tackled. The first is to buy equipment which exceeds the immediate requirements by a factor of, say, two. The second is to buy equipment which can be readily upgraded on site. The third option is to accept that when the need for additional capacity arises a second machine similar to the first will be installed.

The first course may in the long run be the most economical method. It may be substantially cheaper to buy the top of the range initially, than to upgrade to a higher specification later. For example, there may only be a difference in cost of 20% between disk drives of twice that capacity.

The third option, to buy a second completely independent system, exists as a result of the relatively low price of microcomputer hardware. This has the incidental advantage of providing a back-up facility for critical functions. Technology is also appearing which will readily allow intercommunication between separate microcomputers thereby forming local networks.

Local networking of microcomputers

One form of a local microcomputer network is shown in Figure 3. The system consists of a central disk file and program store which will be controlled by a dedicated microcomputer. A cable or 'data highway' from the control micro can be linked to remote microcomputers. The initial system may consist of no more than the central file store, control micro and one remote microcomputer for processing. However, should additional computing power be required it is a simple matter to attach additional microcomputers to the 'data highway', thereby increasing the total processing power. The system works in a similar fashion to a ring main circuit for domestic electricity supply. Thus the central consumer unit provides a cable which loops round the house, with power outlets provided at appropriate points. The consumer is then able to plug in appliances at power points as he chooses and, within reason, where he chooses. With a networked computer system the user is able to plug in additional processing power at any point on the data highway as required.

In operation the remote microcomputers load the appropriate applications program from the central file store and also call up any data files required. All processing and input of additional data then takes place at the remote microcomputer, leaving the file store free to service other users. When processing at the remote microcomputer is finished the updated information is written back to the central file and the task is complete.

The system has two important advantages. Firstly, it allows an increase in computing power as demand increases. Secondly, the system is extremely robust because, with the exception of the central file and control micro, all other components are non-critical. Thus the failure of any of the remote microcomputers does not affect the operation of the remainder. In fact, it would simply be necessary to unplug a faulty microcomputer and replace it with a working unit, or use another machine on the circuit.

Networked microcomputer systems are readily available and will

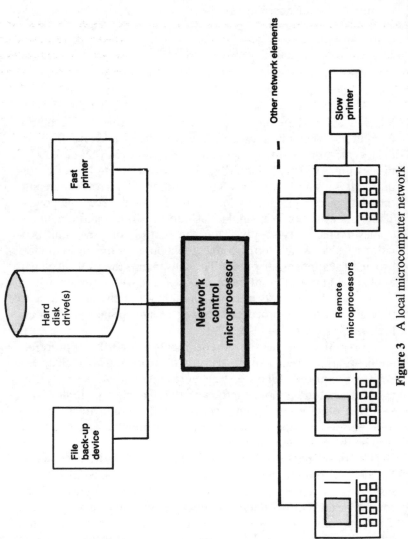

Figure 3 A local microcomputer network

become more widely used in the near future. A networked system offers an elegant and robust solution to the user whose data processing requirements are likely to increase. However, networked systems are still a relatively new concept in data processing and it is not generally recommended that the business user be a guinea pig for a new system. The microcomputer network should be considered as a possible upgrade path for the future.

5

How Computers Process Data

Files, records and fields

The basis of all data processing is the file. The file is simply a collection of records, each record containing information laid out to a common pattern so that the computer can process each one in a common way. This is best illustrated by reference to a simple card index for employees.

In such a card index there is a card for each employee. On each card there is a box for the employee's name, a box for his job description, a box for his date of birth etc. The collection of cards is the *file*, each card is an (employee) *record* and each box contains a common element of information referred to in computer terms as a *field*.

A computer file is held in disk storage as described in the previous chapter and a computer program which uses that file normally has access to one record at a time. The layout of fields on each one is recorded within the program. Thus a payroll program will operate first on the record for the first employee(s), take in all input information (e.g. hours worked, etc), do all the calculations for him and then access the record for the second employee(s) and repeat the process. So that one program can be used for all employees, the layout of fields in each record of any given file is standardised.

In Figure 4, each box represents a space which is available for the recording of a character, that is, a letter, a digit, punctuation mark or sign ($+-$).

These storage spaces are referred to as *bytes*. Storage capacity is stated in terms of bytes.

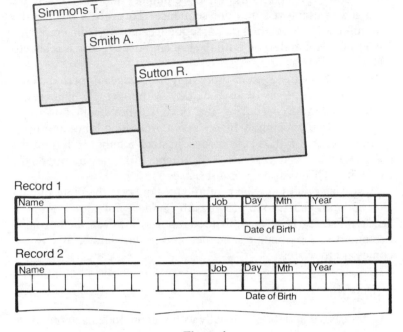

Figure 4

The above explanation is essential to an understanding of data processing.

To recap – the hierarchy is:

1 the file
2 the records
3 the fields – standardised for each record
4 the bytes – the number in any given field may be fixed, or have a maximum value.

The record layout is fixed by the particular program and is in no sense a function of the hardware.

Serial and direct access

The records in a computer file are always held in some specified sequence. In a payroll file, for example, it is usual to have a field in each record which contains employee number and the records are arranged in employee number sequence. To process the file the computer accesses records in that sequence, moving from employee 1 to employee 2 and so on until the last employee record is reached. This is *serial processing*.

In a stock control system there may be changes to perhaps only 5% of the stock items in any one day. Moreover, the changes, if posted as they occur during the day, will not be in any given sequence. In these circumstances serial processing is not appropriate. The records will be held on disk in stock number order but the computer may need to access, say, number 1011 then number 0432 then 0584. This is *random* or *direct access*.

Accessing of files may be required, not only for the input of data (i.e. updating) but also to provide information. For enquiries direct access must clearly be used. Printed reports, however, are normally presented in a particular sequence and sequential processing becomes appropriate.

Updating

The process of updating is usually well understood. Each record to be updated is normally accessed directly and new data is written as appropriate in any field which has changed. Alternatively, in cases where a complete list of entries is required for audit trail purposes, the file is progressively enlarged by appending additional records to the single main file.

In considering updating it is useful to distinguish between standing data and temporary data. Thus in a payroll most of the information about an employee can be regarded as standing data but gross-pay-to-date and tax-to-date will clearly change at each pay calculation. Included in the updating of standing data is the addition of new records to the file and the deletion of records no longer required.

Sorting

Records held in disk storage will be held as stated above in a particular sequence and this sequence will be that of one of the fields, for example, the employee number field for payroll. It is possible, however, that for some types of printed output the records will be required in some other sequence. If, for instance, we have a file of sales invoices for a year, the file may well be held in order of invoice number. In each sales invoice record, however, there may be a field indicating the salesman who obtained the sale. The file may therefore be processed to give another file in salesman number order. It is then a simple task to print all the sales for each salesman in turn to provide appropriate totals. The process of copying the file in a different sequence of records is called sorting.

Sorting can be time consuming on a small machine and sometimes quicker processes may meet the need. For instance, in the example given, if the requirement was simply to know the value of the total sales for each salesman for the year, an analysis could be made by a suitable program without the need to sort the file.

Selecting/comparing

This is a task at which the computer excels. It forms the basis of such apparently diverse requirements as those of the marriage bureau and the estate agent. To the computer the process of looking for a suitable husband is much the same as looking for a suitable house. In the one there will be a file of husband records, in the other a file of house records. Each record will have fields indicating the qualities on which a selection may be required. When a selection is required the criteria of selection in terms of the particular fields will be input and the program will select and print (or display) all the records which meet the criteria.

It is to be noted that the criteria may not demand simply a direct match. The program of selection may allow considerable scope for variation. For example, it may provide for either a 3 or a 4 bedroom house, it may provide for a house value of £40,000 with a tolerance plus or minus of £5,000. It may provide for a husband who is under 40 years of age and who is interested in either music or in drama or both.

Validity tests

The testing of input data against error is a feature of all good input programs. Tests are almost always based on a comparison with data which is carried as constant(s) in the input program or in the file which is being updated. The tests do not guarantee accuracy but do prevent many errors which would otherwise occur. Examples are:

1   The record number for an amend update or a record deletion must correspond with a record number on file. On agreement, the description held on file (e.g. employee name, customer name, stock item description) will be displayed as a check;
2   The record number for a new record must not be held on the file. If it were, two records with the same indicative number would be created;
3   A value must fall within a given range of values as held in the program;
4   An alphabetical code letter must be one which is recorded as permissible in the program;
5   A check digit may be incorporated as the final digit in all account numbers. This is a means of guarding against the transposition or wrong copying of figures during input.

Use of codes

The term *code* in this context means a number such as an account number or a stock item number. To the layman the need to use codes in data processing is annoying. Before a file is updated each item to be posted or each amendment to be made has to bear the appropriate code number, so that this can be input and the correct record accessed. Wherever possible, of course, each input document should be given its code when originated to avoid the need to look it up later. Once the code is on the document the advantage is very real. The operator merely has to input the three, four or five digits of the code and the appropriate account is found. Without a code number the operator would have to input the full title of the account – a much longer task and more prone to error. Without a code there could easily be confusion as a result of imprecise input. Thus if the account were described on the input document as A. Bloggins & Co. but on the computer files as A. B. Bloggins & Co. there would be no match in the computer and the input would have to be rejected.

   Codes are also used with advantage to describe such things as sales areas, package types, etc. when information is required from the computer relating to these items. Care in allocating code numbers, so that new code numbers can be sensibly inserted to avoid ambiguity of meaning, is important in designing computer systems.

Reports and enquiries

The term *report* is loosely applied to any printed output but generally implies a list of items with or without totals based on a particular 'sort' order. Thus a sales report may be presented in order of sales area but within each area totals may be provided in product sequence for each product. There is no great difficulty in programming new types of report but it is of course essential that all the data required in a report should be held in the computer file. Most reports are produced on some regular time cycle, for example each day, each week, each month, each quarter or each year.

Enquiries are requests for information to be printed or to be displayed on the screen. The form of the request has always to be pre-programmed and in order to answer it the appropriate disk must be loaded into the machine. Good application packages contain a variety of possible types of enquiry.

'When I was a lad we just stuck a note up the chimney.'

(*Punch*)

6
Typical
Applications

In this chapter, seven general application areas for business computer use are described and in addition there are discussions of the systems used by insurance brokers, estate agents and hotels. These applications by no means cover the whole field of computing for small business, but they do illustrate many of the basic concepts, advantages and problems of computer use. Those readers who consider their problems unique, may well clarify their thinking by an appreciation of what is involved in these more common applications.

There is no precise definition of a computer application; it is simply an area of work for a computer. Such areas may be thought of in isolation or as standing alone. There is for instance no connection between payroll and engineering calculations and indeed there may be no connection between one engineering calculation and another. Each has its own program or programs and the data used for one may have no connection with the data used in another. In business computing, however, it often happens that the outputs of one application are the inputs to another. Thus the invoice totals from sales invoicing are clearly inputs to sales ledger. In such circumstances sales invoicing and sales ledger may be considered either as one large application or as two applications which are linked or integrated.

For the sake of clarity, computer applications in this chapter are generally described at what can be called the lower level; that is, sales invoicing is described separately from sales ledger. Where appropriate the possibility of links to other applications are mentioned. It should be noted that such links always infer that output from one application is held on computer disk storage so that it can be input to another application without further keying. If the input were printed and then re-keyed as new input there would not be an automatic machine link and the two applications would be considered to be 'stand-alone'. Stand-alone systems are simpler to install and maintain. On the other hand avoidance of extensive re-keying and of errors which can occur in re-keying may point to integration.

Areas of application

The first six application areas have been arranged in what might loosely be described as order of complexity. After the relative simplicity of the mailing list, there follow the difficult but generally well-understood areas of the accounting ledgers (sales, purchase and nominal). The next two applications are stock control and production control. Both these systems have to be closely tied in with the actual operations of the business and because in detail these vary so much from one business to another, the computer systems have to be carefully tailored to conform. The last application is payroll.

In describing each application, a common plan has in general been followed. Comment on the relevance of the application to small business is followed by a description of the principal file used and how it is updated. The more common reports are listed, enquiries via the screen are mentioned and a summary is given of the main benefits and possible problems involved in the application.

The mailing list
The mailing list is not necessarily the same thing as a list of customers. Potential clients of the business or clients who normally purchase through distributors may be included. From the computer viewpoint, however, the list is a file in which each record holds a client's code number, his name, his address and a code or codes, for example geographical area or type of business, on which selection for any particular mailing can be based. Updating of the file consists simply of the addition of new clients, deletion of clients no longer circulated, or amendments to names, addresses and codes.

If sales ledger and/or sales invoicing is a computer application and if mailing is to be confined to existing customers, names and addresses for print labels can be obtained directly from these systems.

The benefit in using a computer for mailing lies in the ease and speed of label printing, in the simplicity of maintaining an up-to-date file and in the convenience of selecting any group of clients for a particular mail shot.

The mailing list is described above as an application in data processing terms. The absence of computation and the simplicity of the processing mean, however, that it can be treated as a word processing application (see also Chapter 11).

The sales ledger

Sales of goods or services are a key element in every business and the due collection of cash from credit sales is essential. It is no accident therefore that sales ledger is one of the most common computer applications. As described below, it excludes sales invoicing.

In a manual or machine posted sales ledger, each customer's record is held as a separate opening in the ledger or on a card. In a computer system, similar information is carried on magnetic disk. Thus each customer's record contains his account number, name and address, credit limit, balance brought forward and the transaction (invoices, credit notes and cash) posted to his account.

Updating this information takes place regularly throughout the month and falls into two broad classes:

1 Amendments of standing information, such as change of a customer address, the insertion of records for new customers or the deletion of records for customers whose accounts are no longer active;
2 The posting of current transactions.

The information concerning any customer account can be displayed on the screen at any time by an enquiry quoting the appropriate account number.

The most troublesome part of the system is normally the allocation of cash received against particular invoices. Where the number of invoices per month for each account is few and payment is normally prompt, it will be sufficient for the computer to carry forward a balance once a month and to offset cash received against this balance (balance forward method). In other circumstances each cash or credit posting made by the operator must quote the relevant invoice numbers so that the computer can tag these in storage. At month end the computer will then bring forward open items in lieu of a balance (the open item method).

The open item method requires more disk storage and in machine terms is rather more complex.

Links to the nominal ledger can be provided by adding a nominal ledger code to each transaction posted. In an integrated sales and nominal ledger package, the appropriate figures will then be automatically posted to the nominal accounts. Otherwise a list of transactions sorted to the nominal ledger code can be printed.

The updating of a sales ledger file as described above is a procedure carried out jointly by operator and computer. Given a computer of adequate capacity, its speed is largely determined by the suitability of the source documents – good document design is important. The merits of using a computer lie in the machine's ability to select and sort the information stored to produce printed reports. In this work the dominant factor is generally the speed of the printer and the operator is little involved.

Reports, which vary considerably in content and format according to the software package used, are:

1 Day book – a list of all transactions with control totals, providing an audit trail;
2 Statements – sometimes accompanied by a remittance advice which, if completed and returned by the customer, simplifies the task of cash allocation;
3 Debtors' list – a list showing aged balances and indicating those debtors who have exceeded their credit control limit;
4 Customers' lists and printed labels – in respect of all customers or on a selective basis.

To the small business, savings in clerical effort provided by a computerised sales ledger are unlikely to be significant. A valuable improvement in cash flow may, however, be achieved by the prompt production of statements at the end of the month (or other accounting period) together with the tight control afforded by use of the debtors' list.

Purchase ledger

The purchase ledger has obvious similarities to the sales ledger. In place of a customer file there is a supplier file and this is updated in much the same way, that is by the entry of amendments and by the posting of transactions.

Before purchase invoices are entered via the keyboard, it is necessary to check them for accuracy, possibly classify them for nominal ledger/cost centre, and to decide whether the payment date and amount is to be varied from the normal method specified for the computer.

Software packages normally offer various options for the running of the system and these options may – according to the package chosen – apply to all suppliers or to particular suppliers. Among these options are:

1 Open item or balance forward method – in other words, whether separate details are to be held on file of all old unpaid invoices or merely a balance is to be carried forward at month end;
2 Payment date to be determined by the computer based on standing rules and information held for each supplier or following clerical inspection of a computer-produced list of payments due;
3 Payment amount to be calculated by the computer from the amounts due less available discounts or clerically following inspection;
4 Whether there is to be an analysis of invoices for the nominal ledger and whether the posting to that ledger will be carried out automatically by the computer;
5 Whether the system is to produce credit transfers for suppliers who opt for this method rather than payment by cheque.

Reports which are normally produced by the system are:

1 Day book – A list of invoices posted together with totals for VAT and control;
2 Payment – Remittance advice accompanied by a cheque or credit transfer;
3 Payment list – In effect this constitutes the cash book entries for the purchase ledger;

4   Nominal ledger analysis – At the end of the accounting period the system may list all invoices by nominal account with totals so that the nominal ledger may be posted manually if this is not to be done automatically by computer.

The main merit of transferring the purchase ledger to a computer is the ability to exercise tight control over payments and thus optimise cash resources. It also permits allocation of costs to be kept accurately in step with expenditure, with minimum effort.

The nominal ledger
The nominal or general ledger provides an accounting summary of all activities, assets and liabilities of a business. Thus income is analysed by source (e.g. sales, rent receivable). Expenditure is analysed by type (e.g. purchases for stock, wages, insurance). For each analysis head an account is opened and transactions are posted to these accounts, either as they occur or as periodic totals from subsidiary books.

Some small businesses do not maintain a nominal ledger. A retailer, for instance, may make all his sales for cash and he may consider that he can keep adequate control of his business by analysing his purchases and other expenditure under relatively few heads. He keeps a record of all cash movements and of any payments or receipts due. From these records his accountant is able to construct summary accounts for the year. Thus the accountant in effect constructs a nominal ledger.

In a computer system for a nominal ledger, the basic record is a nominal account and at the beginning of an accounting period each record will simply have an account number, description and opening balance stored on disk. To this record transactions will be posted in the way described for sales ledger. As each transaction is posted a new balance is computed and the transaction with the latest balance is stored on disk.

The need for separate manual postings for sales and purchases can be obviated if the nominal ledger is run on a software package which permits integration with the sales ledger and purchase ledger. In such a system postings to these two ledgers will contain the appropriate nominal ledger account number so that the computer can automatically post them to the nominal ledger.

For businesses which operate more than one department, separate accounts may be opened for each (e.g. Sales Department A, Sales Department B). Expenditure in so far as it can be allocated to departments may be similarly split. This creates the opportunity for preparing periodic operating statements for each department – obviously at a cost in disk storage space and in computer time. In addition budgeted amounts for each department may be input and stored to provide variance figures on the operating statement.

Reports provided by the system are:

1   Transactions list – gives a record of each day's transactions as recorded in the system;
2   Trial balance – provides verification that debits and credits are in fact in balance; gives totals on each account for the period and hence provides an overall view of the state of business; can be produced at any time;
3   Nominal ledger details – a complete list of all transactions for audit purposes;
4   Operating statement – a monthly, quarterly or annual statement showing expenditure by type and, where required, variances from budget.

A decision to use a computer for the nominal ledger will depend on the complexity of the business, in other words on the volume of transactions and the degree of analysis required for business control. The posting of the accounts and adjustments for errors and omissions require a more formal approach than in the manual system.

The speed of establishing a trial balance and the ease and frequency with which the financial state of the business may be ascertained are, however, major benefits. In a business of any complexity these advantages far outweigh other factors, particularly where the purchase and nominal ledgers are implemented as an integrated computer system.

Sales order/invoicing

There is a natural order of progression from sales order to sales invoice to sales ledger. These three areas are obviously linked and it is possible to enter the computer system at any of the three stages, in other words on receipt of an order, at the invoicing stage, or simply for production of the sales ledger. Thus there are three broad possibilities for computer use:

1   Sales ledger only;
2   Sales invoicing with sales ledger;
3   Order processing with sales invoicing and sales ledger.

Sales ledger was considered in an earlier section of this chapter. Sales invoicing is now considered and this is followed by a consideration of various possibilities which arise in order processing.

For the production of sales invoices two files are required – the customer file and the product file. As required for invoicing purposes, each customer record need contain no more than the customer's account number, his name and address and coded information relating to his contract price. Since the same file will be used for sales ledger purposes it will also contain particulars of past invoices and payments.

The product file will contain a record of each type of product/package, according to the way it is sold and invoiced (e.g. gloss paint, red, 1 litre tins). Each record will contain a product code, product description and price.

As goods are despatched, consignment particulars are keyed in, the operator entering first the customer code, then the product code and quantity for each line of the invoice. As each entry is made, the screen displays the appropriate descriptions for a check of the accuracy of the keying. The full invoice is thus built up on the screen for storage on the disk and for immediate or subsequent printing.

In deciding the feasibility of computer use for sales invoicing, there are two interrelated key points. The first is the definition of the units of sale, in other words the product/packages or equivalent. The second is the method of pricing. It is essential that there should be a logical and unvarying definition of the units of sale and that this should be consistent with any system of stock control.

Pricing has to be based on standing information carried in the product and the customer files. If, for instance, the unit price depends simply on the quantity ordered, it can be deduced from information in the product file. Again if customers fall into say three contract groups, each group having its own discount rate, a group code can be stored in the individual customer record. From this code the discount rate can be applied to the product price to give the price for that customer.

Program packages of course vary in the pricing facilities they offer and selection of a package will depend on its suitability for the business requirements. All packages, however, have to be based on some logical pricing structure. If such a structure does not exist, in other words if prices for each product are individually negotiated with each customer, computer pricing is unlikely to be a practical proposition. In such circumstances a consultant's advice should be sought.

Order processing can be considered in three contexts:

1   Where goods are not available for immediate despatch and a simple progressing system is required;
2   Where goods are always held in stock and an integrated order/stock control/sales invoice system is required;
3   Where goods are manufactured to order and integration of sales orders with production control is required.

The implications of the last two approaches can be recognised by reading the sections in this chapter on stock control and production control. An integrated order/stock control/sales invoicing system is an ambitious project for a small business, demanding a careful system study and thorough investigation of the facilities offered by appropriate program packages. These remarks apply with even greater force where there is to be integration with production control.

In contrast with these fairly complex approaches, progressing orders need involve little more than is required for sales invoicing. It is, of course, possible to produce a despatch set by computer, that is to print an order and an invoice at the same time. The invoice copy is then held in the accountancy section until the order copy is returned signifying that the goods have been despatched. Alternatively, as each order is received, order documents may be produced and full data concerning the order placed in disk storage, pending notification of despatch. Entry of the appropriate order number on the computer will then call forward all information from the disk storage for the printing of the invoice and posting of the sales ledger. This latter system provides an open order file, which can be interrogated by screen enquiry as necessary to show the current order position.

Stock control

Not all small businesses have stock control problems and for those that do the computer may not provide a suitable answer. In order to understand the issues involved in this question, it is first necessary to consider the possible objects of a system of stock control and then to consider how far each may be met by a computer in the circumstances of the particular business. The possible objects are:

1 To enable stock holdings and movements to be reviewed to minimise the capital tied up in stock;
2 To indicate the need to re-order – this demands not only an up-to-date knowledge of stock levels but also of the current rate of usage and delivery lead times;
3 To indicate stock availability without the need to examine physical stock, such as in answer to a customer's telephone call or when drawing up a production programme based on components held in stock;
4 To maintain an accounting record to ascertain stock values and as a deterrent to pilferage.

Some small businesses with few stock lines may be able to maintain adequate control by visual check of stock, coupled with minimum accounting records. Some retailers with a variety of selling lines may feel the need for stock control but would find the bookings of individual sales to any form of stock record quite impractical. Any system of stock control has, therefore, to be designed to accord with the requirements of the business and with the practical operating situation. Clerical systems may be designed to meet all four of the objectives given above or simply some of them.

The majority of computer stock control systems are able to meet all four. Even so there is considerable variety in the facilities offered by the various packages and before contacting suppliers the businessman needs to consider:

1 Whether the system is to cover raw materials, sub-assemblies or finished goods, or more than one of these;

2   Whether some items are collections of other items and what should be the stock unit(s) in these circumstances;
3   Whether it is desirable to record items in groups so as to allow, for example, price changes to be made by groups rather than by individual stock items;
4   Whether all items of stock are to be treated by the computer in the same way (e.g. in relation to re-ordering);
5   Whether there is to be automatic linkage by the computer to the sales invoice package or a production control package.

These are quite broad questions important in the choice of system.

The basis of any computer system for stock control is the stock file. This consists of a record for every stock item and each record holds stock item number, description, actual stock held, re-order level, re-order quantity, cost price, and so on. According to the purposes for which it is to be used and the particular program package chosen, each record may also contain a retail price, a supplier's code, stock allocations, quantity on order and total of stock issues during the current month and year. The system may also contain the supplier's name and address file to facilitate the printing of orders to suppliers.

Updating this file in respect of receipts, issues and returns to stock has to be carried out on a regular daily basis and a well-organised, disciplined procedure for doing this and for making any required changes in standing data is essential. Without such an approach, the file information will rapidly get out of step with the actual stock position and become useless or positively misleading.

Reports produced by a full computer system for stock control typically include:

1 Complete (or by section) list of stock items with information as stored in the computer;
2 Orders print – prints orders where replenishment is required according to the rules given in the particular program package;
3 Activity report – analyses movements for management reassessment of order levels, etc., and for audit purposes.

From the foregoing, it will be appreciated that there is no one optimal file nor one optimal system for stock control, for the information required will depend on the needs of the business. Many packages offer a wide choice of facilities but this is not necessarily advantageous from the user's point of view. A package which includes many facilities not required by the user, will be unnecessarily complex and is likely to make undue demands on computer capacity and file space – in other words longer operating times and higher costs than necessary.

While the system of stock control chosen must accord with the real needs of the business, it would be unwise to assume that this implies a slavish copy of an existing clerical system. The computer offers great advantages over manual systems but these advantages can only be realised if the system is seen as a joint manual and computer system. A willingness to move away from old ideas and to see the problems afresh is necessary. Given this approach, a move from manual to joint manual and computer stock control is likely to result in lower clerical costs, better control, and a reduction of the working capital required.

Production control

The term *production control* is a convenient label for a great variety of planning, monitoring and efficiency-reporting systems. The possible differences are augmented by the fact that these systems may or may not involve an important element of stock control at various stages of production. The variety originates, of course, from the great diversity of products and manufacturing methods used in modern industry. The general label, however, all too easily masks this variety and may suggest to the unwary that a program package for production control will meet the requirements of any situation. This is not so; package selection should not be made until the real production problems have been carefully analysed.

Many program packages are available for production control and each package consists of a number of modules which can be grouped to suit the particular situation. Despite the modular approach, the volume of sales for any package is relatively small, when compared with popular packages such as sales ledger, and for this reason prices are high. For a comprehensive system a typical price would be £10,000 but cheaper packages are available. However, when the requirements have been well analysed a suitable computer system for production control may well offer far greater benefits than the more conventional accounting applications.

The broad questions to be asked in considering production control are as follows:

1 What are the production stations and how are they related in terms of product and work flow? A clear answer to this question, probably in diagrammatic form, is an essential preliminary to clarifying the nature of the problem;

2 Is the production system best seen as a flowline where the problem is to ensure efficiency in each section so that the flow as a whole is maintained? This is a progress type problem and microprocessor control of plant may be applicable;

3 Is the problem a matter of hour-by-hour control or rather one of planning on a day-by-day or weekly basis? The type of system is likely to depend heavily on this question;

4 Does production take the form of batch production at various stages with intermediate stocks? If so, does the problem consist mainly of maintaining adequate stocks at each stage, in other

words is the problem really a series of stock control problems for which a stock control package may be adequate?

5   Is there a need for requirements planning, that is of forward ordering to ensure parts are available for each production run? In so far as a list of parts can be standardised for each assembly or finished item, a computer can be particularly useful (the parts explosion module);

6   Is the problem really a need for order monitoring to ensure that all orders are progressed smoothly through each stage of production and that delays are quickly identified? This is a relatively simple and low cost application.

When an answer to these questions is obtained there follows the all important question as to how far a solution should be sought by operator or manager's calculations and how far by use of a computer. Initially it may well pay to be cautious and to attempt a computer solution in strictly limited problem areas. The more comprehensive systems are likely to prove unduly costly for a small business and in some circumstances use of a small computer locally programmed for specific tasks may prove a sensible approach. An example of production records is given in Case Studies, under Company ADD.

Payroll
Justification for using a computer for payroll is almost invariably based on reduction of clerical costs. If the number of employees is small, then buying a computer solely for payroll is unlikely to be justified.

A record is held in disk storage for every employee and this contains standing information (e.g. employee number, name, tax code, standing deductions from pay) together with tax brought forward (gross pay to date and tax to date). In order that the computer may calculate gross pay the standing information will include as appropriate the annual salary, the hourly rate, shift allowance, and so on.

For those employees with no change of circumstances since the last payment – and this is normal for salaried staff – no input is required. Any changes, including hours worked for hourly paid staff, have of course to be keyed in and should be subjected to validity tests. Apparent errors are displayed on the screen for immediate correction. On completion of this updating the computer calculates gross pay, National Insurance contributions, tax and net pay, and updates the standing information with the new gross pay to date and tax to date.

Reports from the system consist, of course, of pay slips and payroll together with a coin analysis or list of bank credits as appropriate. A cost analysis may also be provided according to cost centre data, if this is carried as standing information in the employer's record. At the end of the tax year the computer has all the necessary data to print P60 forms and the Inland Revenue return.

Before choosing a software package for payroll it will be necessary to specify requirements which will include not only the method of calculating gross pay but the number of non-taxable additions to pay, the number of standard and special deductions and any savings schemes in respect for instance of holiday pay.

The main saving in clerical effort arises primarily from the automatic repetition of all unchanged data from one pay calculation to the next and from the automatic calculation of tax without clerical reference to tax brought forward and to tax tables. Two provisos need, however, to be made. First, as a precaution against some form of system failure, the computer operations should preferably be scheduled to take place one day before results are required. Second, in a small firm, the need for privacy may require that the actual work be carried out by the proprietor or a senior member of staff.

Insurance brokers

Insurance, as a business which is heavily dependent on clerical records, has long been seen as an area for profitable computer use. It is only in recent years, however, that low cost systems suitable for use by small brokerage firms have become available. Various software packages are obtainable and in the UK the British Insurance Brokers Association (BIBA) has been active in assisting systems development.

A principal feature of insurance broking is that each business transaction (e.g. new policy or policy renewal) has two aspects: it is both a 'sale' to the customer and a 'purchase' from the company providing the insurance. This twin aspect can be readily covered by the computer from a single posting entry – a very significant advantage when compared with the normal clerical method.

More important, however, are the possible advantages to be gained in business control as illustrated by the more commonly produced reports:

1 Ledgers (client, purchase and nominal as described in other sections);
2 Premium and claim analysis for each class of business;
3 Business achieved by individual salesmen;
4 Brokerage earned analysis.
5 Management of clients' portfolios (Bonds).

Other systems may be aimed to support the salesman and hence to expand business:

6 Mailing list;
7 Print of individual client policies showing renewal dates and indirectly indicating to the salesman possible scope for new business.

There is also within insurance broking a need for semi-repetitive typing and hence scope for word processing.

Estate agents

Computer applications which are of interest to estate agents are property matching, and accounting which sometimes includes estate management. The principles used by a computer for matching client requirements with available properties are similar for residential and commercial property but differ in detail. The greater demand is for residential property and the matching system for this is described below. Some differences in the information carried would be required for commercial property.

The property file consists of a record for each available property and each record contains separate fields for items such as location, asking price, detached/semi/terraced/end terraced, number of living rooms, number of bedrooms, freehold/leasehold/rented, garage, garden size, type of central heating. Further fields may be allocated for the date property is entered on file and for the number of enquiries received. The file is, of course, updated as necessary to include 'new' properties or for adjustments, for example, in respect of asking price, or for entry of an 'under offer' signal.

A similar file may be created for the potential buyers but the information contained will normally be less specific; for example, a client may not have a requirement in regard to central heating and the price might be a range or a maximum. The less specific a buyer's requirements, the greater will be the number of properties matched by the computer.

The most obvious use for the system is to display or have printed a list of properties in response to a new client's enquiry. By creating a file of potential buyers, however, it is immediately possible to select buyers who may be interested in a 'new property'. Other reports which may be available under the program package are:

1   Properties in price order;
2   Properties offered to buyers/properties under offer/properties with no buyers, etc.

Accounting applications for estate agents may include the purchase and nominal ledgers as described above. Accounting required for estate management is more specialised. The file for such a system has a record for each property with fields for property address, rent amount, rates, service charges, insurance, tenant's account number, rent review date, and so on.

Typically, a computer system for estate management would be able to produce the following reports:

1   Rent demands;
2   Arrears letters;
3   Lists of rents received and rents due;
4   Analysis of service charges, insurance, etc.;
5   Various lists of summaries, for example tenants' balances, VAT payments, properties vacant, properties for rent review.

The overall range of applications for estate agents, embracing commercial and industrial property matching, accounting and estate management, is wide and the facilities offered by suppliers vary greatly. System prices (hardware plus software) vary similarly but lie generally in the range of £5,000 to £50,000.

Hotels

The range of computer applications available to hotels is wide. As well as applications such as purchase ledger, payroll and stock control (bar stocks) which have been described in preceding sections, there is 'front office' accounting, comprising room reservations and guest accounts. Guest accounts may include not only room and meal charges but charges for drinks and hotel-shop purchases. This area of work is of obvious importance and the speed and efficiency with which it is carried out is an important element in guest service.

Records within the computer system for the front office are defined by room number. For each room number a forward diary can be held showing reservations made and, vice versa, accommodation available. It is updated as bookings or cancellations are received and will provide up-to-date information via the screen of rooms available.

The room charge may be recorded in each room record as standing data or be input for each guest. As each guest checks in, his name is confirmed against the room number reservation. Subsequently the room charge (inclusive of meals if appropriate) is automatically entered by computer each day until check-out. Purchases of additional meals, drinks, etc., are entered from signed chits as soon as possible so that an up-to-date record for each guest is maintained. There is provision for a change of room during a guest's stay and erroneous entries can be deleted.

Comprehensive systems for the front office provide printed documents as follows:

1   Bill for each guest at check-out, including VAT, service charge (if required), less any prepaid deposit;
2   List of rooms to be vacated on the following morning;
3   Analysis of day's business including payments received;
4   Exceptions note to highlight excessive bills or people who have not checked out when expected.

A computer system for front office accounting demands less clerical effort than other systems partly because of the automatic recording of room charges each day and partly because brought-forward sub-totals do not have to be input prior to each clerical entry. Client bills can be displayed at any time on the screen and printed bills have the merit of not showing repeated sub-totals. Overall a major benefit of computer use is that one piece of equipment, suitably specified, can be used for various front office tasks and for various other accounting tasks including the ledgers and payroll.

7

Suppliers and Sources of Advice

Introduction

The current situation in respect of microcomputer suppliers is best understood by considering the history of the microcomputer over the past year or two. When microcomputers were first introduced to the UK market they were promoted as personal computers, for use at home by the individual hobbyist or enthusiast. Software was virtually non-existent and many of the earlier designs of micro-computer had features such as small calculator-type keyboards or were restricted to cassette storage mechanisms.

These early home computers matured into machines which were presented more professionally, with conventional typewriter keyboards and floppy disk storage mechanisms, and became suit-able tools for business use. Such machines are now sold for a capital cost of about £1,500 and this low cost has resulted in an explosive growth in sales.

This growth in sales (major distributors are now selling more than a thousand machines per month) has produced two unfortunate consequences. Firstly, the hardware is ahead of the software, and while the hardware can on the whole justifiably be described as extremely good, the same cannot be said of much of the software. Secondly, with computer systems costing so little, the only essential requirement for establishing oneself as a microcomputer dealer is to be able to purchase one or two systems, with minimal capital investment. This has resulted in a proliferation of suppliers, many of whom were selling electrical consumer goods prior to the move into computers and who may not have the necessary experience to provide sound advice and a proper maintenance service to the business user.

In consideration of the above information it should be obvious that the prospective purchaser must be wary when assessing suppliers, and while there are no doubt some excellent small dealers who are able to provide a thorough, personal service, there are many who do not.

The remainder of this chapter summarises the different types of supplier and provides information on other sources of assistance. This information is necessarily generalised and there are of course always exceptions, both good and bad. The old maxim 'let the buyer beware' is particularly appropriate and there really is no substitute for thorough preparation and analysis of requirements. It is essential to leave as little to chance as possible and to accept nothing at face value, but to make thorough checks on all claims and promises. In particular, the buyer should be extremely wary of the claim 'available in a few weeks' as such elusive products frequently fail to materialise at all. Under no circumstances should a commitment be made for a system which has not been adequately demonstrated.

Original equipment manufacturers (OEM)

The established names in larger computer systems normally manufacture, market and service their own hardware and software. These manufacturers have a well-organised sales force with local offices throughout the country and the back-up of a team of service engineers who will be thoroughly conversant with the computer systems for which they are responsible.

The maintenance of such marketing and service teams is extremely expensive and has to be paid for. In consequence the cost of systems from OEMs is generally higher than alternative sources and it is largely a business decision for the prospective purchaser to weigh the service offered against the price.

Microcomputer dealers

Microcomputer dealers vary from an essentially one man business to a local branch of an organisation with outlets nationwide. In fact one of the major high street electrical retailers has recently started

COMPUTER SALES

'Bad news, Partridge – the computers can sell themselves now.'

(Punch)

selling microcomputers in major cities throughout the country. In most cases dealers will buy hardware from the manufacturers or through their importers and sell direct to the public. As a consequence of the rapidly increasing demand for the small business computer, popular microcomputers effectively sell themselves. Many dealers have found that they cannot get hold of stocks fast enough. This is not an unhappy situation for the dealer, but it can lead to problems for the buyer.

It has been repeatedly stressed in this book that the intending buyer should start with an assessment of software. Unfortunately many people new to computing start with the computer and may end up with impressive hardware systems slowly gathering dust because of the absence of suitable software. The prospective pur-

chaser is therefore recommended to satisfy himself that the dealer
provides an acceptable level of expertise and service in the following
categories:

1   An understanding of business practice;
2   The ability to assess the user's likely requirements for file
    storage and computing capacity;
3   A thorough working knowledge of both software and hardware
    being supplied;
4   A good service record;
5   Adequate stocks.

It is worth commenting on the developments that have taken
place at the very bottom end of the computer market. Continuing
advances in technology have made it possible for small, home
computers such as the Sinclair ZX81 to be offered for under £39
(1984 prices). This has resulted in a much increased level of sales,
both to the hobbyist and to the teenager studying computing at
school. In fact the emergence of this type of hobby computer has
created the mail-order computer business – a concept that would
have been unthinkable a few years ago.

A consequence of this surge of interest in very cheap computers
may prove beneficial to the business user. It is likely that many small
dealers will move towards the hobby market, attracted by the rapid
turnover of stock and the very much simpler servicing requirements. Thus it is likely that a division will occur between the dealer
aiming at the consumer and those marketing computer systems for
the business user. It is also probable that the larger dealers will
move towards the systems house approach to computing and will
provide complete turn-key solutions to business problems.

Systems houses and software houses

Systems houses provide complete tailored systems to suit an individual client's requirements. Until recently the type of computer
system supplied would typically be minicomputer based, with
perhaps multiple terminals, providing data processing facilities for a
number of departments in a medium sized company. The high cost
of developing such systems would make it unlikely that small
businesses could consider this type of approach.

Some systems houses have recently begun to provide packaged options for microcomputers and while these are still likely to be expensive compared with what might be offered by a dealer, the experience of the systems house should ensure a professional approach to the task.

Systems houses sometimes provide consultancy advice and this advice may prove useful to the first-time computer user. However, it should be remembered that many systems houses have built their reputation on minicomputers and it would be unwise to engage a consultant who has no experience of the type of computer or the scale of business under consideration.

Software houses in general have a great deal of practical experience of designing systems and providing programs for individual clients, or on a sub-contracted basis, for original equipment manufacturers. However, because of the considerable expense involved in both manpower and equipment, most software houses restrict themselves to a very limited range of equipment and applications. This is not necessarily a bad thing, since nobody can be an expert on everything, and at least by concentrating on a limited range of applications and hardware, a software house should develop competence in that particular field. However, the first time user considering an approach to a software house should be aware of this, since it is only to be expected that the software house will try and provide a system based on equipment with which it is familiar. The comments made on the experience of systems houses applies equally to the traditional software house and similar caution is advised.

Other sources of advice

Accountants

Many of the larger accountancy practices have been involved with computing for a number of years and may offer a consultancy service. Their experience is likely to be broadly based, extending from large mainframe installations to minicomputer systems, but it is unlikely that many firms of accountants will have a great deal of experience with microcomputers.

Nevertheless, the standards and ethical code demanded by the profession mean that such a source of advice is likely to be safe, though possibly somewhat on the cautious side. It is recommended that any manager of a small business who is considering computerisation should thoroughly discuss the matter with his own accountant.

Independent Consultants

This category covers both individuals and companies providing a source of consultancy advice on aspects of computerisation. Reputable consultants are likely to be members of one of the professional associations and should have relevant professional qualifications. Before engaging a consultant it is vital to obtain information on the quality of advice provided and this is best done by contacting a number of his previous clients.

There are consultants claiming to provide a free and independent service to customers. Their services are financed by obtaining a commission on systems purchased as a result of their assessment and recommendation. As with any consultant it is important to establish their level of competence and experience before entering into a commitment.

Universities, polytechnics and colleges

Many universities, polytechnics and colleges have established units which specialise in providing advice to industry and commerce. Such units may be in the form of a separate limited liability company or may simply be an informal grouping of members of staff, with central coordination. Where such units have been providing consultancy in the area of business computing, they are likely to offer a sound source of independent advice to the smaller business.

Additionally, it is not generally recognised by the public that many universities and colleges actively encourage staff to become involved with industry and commerce, and the manager of a small business is always free to make a direct approach to his local college. It should be remembered, however, that practical experience is essential when assisting with a small business application and, as with the professional consultant, care should be taken to ensure that the academic in question has that necessary experience.

The local university or college is also likely to provide a range of short courses which could provide suitable background information for the manager of a small business.

8

Selecting the System and Supplier

How to select

Business proprietors, directors and managers become interested in computing for a variety of reasons. Business expansion or a change in market conditions may give rise to new problems not previously met, sometimes it is found that a competitor has installed a computer, or alternatively a television programme or a chance discussion with a computer enthusiast may generate an idea. Whatever the cause may be, it is important at an early stage to formulate ideas on the subject in a coherent manner, recognising that investment in a computer is not only a significant financial decision but that the larger systems will inevitably involve changes in the jobs that staff do and quite possibly in the way the company works. The project deserves time, thought and a logical approach. These factors have already been stressed in Chapter 1.

The approach will vary according to the nature of the work which the computer is to do and the resources available – primarily management time. It has already been explained how these may point to the use of a computer bureau (see Chapter 2). If on the other hand an in-house system is favoured, a second question has to be faced. Is the computer to be installed to do work in a particular problem area of the business or is the intention to install a more general business system with several areas of application?

A computer which is installed to serve a particular area of the business can be viewed as almost a personal tool for the manager responsible for that area. He may use it to carry out technical or business calculations, to store and retrieve records or to provide statistics. He may use packaged programs, write his own programs or use a mixture of both. The essential point, however, is that the computer is being used in a sense as his personal assistant and he will personally develop ideas as to what it is to do. Thus the work will be more easily defined and the ability of particular software and equipment to meet his requirements will be more readily assessed than with a more general business system. It follows that the process of selection can be carried out more quickly. Moreover, the capital investment for the personal system might well be less than a quarter of the cost of a general system.

The steps in computer selection described in this chapter are those appropriate to a general system for a small business. They are detailed and demanding of management time. The effort involved would hardly be appropriate to a personal system. This is not to say that the manager who wants to set up a personal system should ignore them, for the differences are of degree rather than of principle. He can, however, adopt a less formal approach and get started more rapidly.

The stages recommended are divided between this and the next chapter. In this chapter we consider how to:

1   Analyse the problems
2   List the application areas
3   Produce a requirements statement
4   Select possible suppliers
5   Call for proposals

Then, in Chapter 9, we look at the following stages:

6   The basic choice
7   Plan and budget
8   Negotiate the contract
9   Install, set up and train
10   Parallel run, go operational

The time spent on each stage will vary according to the business problems and the experience of the director involved in the project. None of the stages, however, calls for a technical knowledge of computing. The emphasis throughout is on careful analysis of business problems and on commonsense, step-by-step solutions. The intention is to remove the mystery of computing and to reduce the various aspects of computer installation to terms of normal business planning.

Analyse the problems

The purpose of this stage is to clarify the business aims, say over the next three years, the problems involved in attaining these aims and to consider whether these problems should or could be met other than by the use of a computer. If there is a problem in handling the volume of paper work with existing staff, if information which is important to the running of the business is not readily available, if it is felt that better information should lead to greater efficiency in stock control, in collecting cash from debtors or in some aspect of production, then there may be justification for a computer. But before the thinking turns to a computer it is important to record the current problems and any new problems which might arise as the aims of the business develop.

There is no doubt that the discipline of noting and recording business aims and probable problem areas is conducive to clear thinking. It also means that as views develop there can be reference back to the record and if necessary amendment of it. Without this discipline it is all too easy to go round in circles and after two months of speculation to be little further forward. This is particularly true for the director of a small business who generally finds that any attempt to think a year or two ahead is certain to be interrupted by the pressing problems of today or tomorrow.

With the aims and problems clearly recorded the next step is to consider whether a clean-up of clerical systems is all that is really required. The views of staff on unnecessary paperwork may be helpful or it may be desirable to seek an outside view. If, despite these measures, the problems seem to point to the use of a computer, there will at least be in outline a basic statement of what it is hoped the computer will achieve.

Before beginning to think more definitely of what the computer is to do, there is a need to know broadly what can be done. Chapters 5 and 6, and the case studies, were written for this purpose. They form a foundation which can be built on by visits to appropriate computer users. A one day computer appreciation course or a course of about five evenings in programming will also assist. The merit of a short programming course lies not in any programming skill which it may confer but, by the actual use of a small computer, computing concepts which are only vaguely appreciated when read about, become clearer and sharper. It is still unnecessary and to some extent harmful to become committed to computing technicalities. There are broader and more important issues to consider.

List the application areas

As a result of the gathering of ideas in stage 1, it should be possible to list the application areas for computer use and to know the type of benefit each may bring. The list should be comprehensive. If, because of uncertain benefits or apparent complexity, there are doubts regarding any area, the area should be included but the doubts should be noted for consideration at a later stage. They may have an important bearing on later discussions. If, for instance, there appears a good argument for computer use in the accounting area but uncertainty regarding production control, it would be unwise to select a supplier who although experienced in accounting, could not offer support for the more uncertain but possibly far more rewarding area of production control.

The recommendation that the list be comprehensive does not in any sense imply that subsequent planning should embrace all areas in detail. There should be gaps, possibly of several months, between converting the various application areas to the computer, allowing time for each to bed down. Indeed there may be a need to enhance the hardware as applications are added. The ideal solution would be to acquire software and hardware for one or two initial applications but to know that there is a growth path available for all possible applications. Unless all the possible applications are listed the need for a growth path may be overlooked and decisions taken which preclude it.

Produce a requirements statement

Following decisions as to the probable application areas, the next step is to draw up a requirements statement. This is in no sense a technical document. It is simply a description of the business, presented in a way which is useful to computer suppliers. A

company able to produce such a statement is well on the road to having proposals submitted.

In some respects the statement of requirements is a broad description and in others it is very detailed. The detailed aspects may well be prepared by an assistant under suitable direction. Some care is needed to ensure that when stating the underlying facts regarding the business and defining requirements, current methods are not necessarily regarded as sacrosanct. If a computer is ordered and a poor manual system is transferred to it, the chances are that the same old fault will arise.

The statement of requirements consists of:

1 A brief description of the business, indicating its activities, the number of people employed, the sites used and any unusual features in its mode of operation;
2 A list of the computer applications, distinguishing between those it is hoped to implement in the first year or two years and those which are regarded as longer term;
3 Detailed information regarding each application for early implementation viz data to be carried in the computer files, the

volumes of data to be processed, the reports required and special rules for which provision is needed.

It should be recognised that this does not constitute a full specification of the work the programs will be required to do. It is basic information required by any supplier who has to recommend suitable software and equipment and should lead rapidly to useful discussion with suppliers about possible ways of meeting the requirements.

The detailed information to be provided for each of the initial applications is:

Data to be carried
This is best expressed by naming the fields to be carried in each record of the master file(s). Thus for sales invoicing the customer file will have fields for customer code, customer name and address, credit limit, sales area, contract terms, balance forward, etc., and the product file will have product code, product name, basic price, etc. As a check, every output document in the existing manual system should be scrutinised to see that all items shown on it are covered by the fields named. The maximum number of characters required in each field should also be noted as many of the cheaper systems severely restrict the amount of space. Once a computer system is set up it is relatively easy to alter the form and contents of an output (printed or displayed) but costly and difficult to change the master file contents. A full list of master file contents for each application is, therefore, particularly important.

Volumes of data
The number of records to be held in each file (e.g. of customers in the customer file) should be stated together with any foreseeable increase. Similarly the number of transactions to be handled daily, weekly or monthly should be given plus possible increases.

Reports required
The name and frequency (daily, weekly, monthly, annually) of each report should be given and if the contents are not obvious from the description, comment should be made. Enquiries which the system will be expected to answer by screen display or print should be listed with permissible time allowance or response.

Special rules, facilities and exceptions
These should be listed so that they are not subsequently over-looked. It would be preferable to define them precisely but this may sometimes be done more readily after discussion with suppliers concerning the options in existing program packages. Exceptions to the rules generally followed by the company are particularly important for they may not be covered by an otherwise satisfactory package. Production control descriptions should be augmented by diagrams which show the relationship and flows of the various products and processes.

Codes
Any codes used for classifying customers, products or processes should be described in outline.

It must be emphasised that the statement of requirements, as described, is by no means a full specification of the computing to be done. It has, however, very definite merits:

1 Its preparation obliges the director responsible to think through the problems facing the company and this will start to clarify ideas about computer use;
2 Its preparation does not require professional computer expertise;
3 It will save time taken in repeated answering of basic questions which every supplier should ask;
4 If consultants are to be used it will reduce the time they require and hence their charges;
5 Above all it will, as far as practically possible for the small business, ensure that subsequent discussions and decisions within the company and with the suppliers are soundly based. It also puts the emphasis on software rather than hardware requirements.

Once the statement of requirements has been produced it should be agreed by interested parties within the company. The way is then clear to approach suppliers either directly or through the use of consultants.

Select possible suppliers

Before contacting possible suppliers, the question of using consultants should be considered. Consultants may, of course, conduct a full investigation but their costs will then be high. By introducing them at this stage their time and cost will be minimised. Consultants can assist by providing:

1   Ability to make useful comment on the project with a minimum of bias towards the computer solution;
2   Ability to clarify problems, to add usefully to the outline of requirements and in particular to advise where changes of system are thought necessary;
3   Knowledge of software and its quality;
4   Knowledge of local suppliers and their ability to support both suitable software and hardware.

It is important that the consultant should act independently of any supplier and a written statement from the consultant to this effect is advisable. When using a consultant it is very desirable to provide him with a clear remit and to receive if possible a fixed price quotation.

The key point in selecting a supplier lies in the choice of suitable software. The choice of hardware is not so significant, provided it is known to work satisfactorily with the chosen software. This point is obscured by two facts. Firstly, the software price is likely to be only a small fraction of the hardware price and hence the importance of software is likely to be underrated. Secondly, there is great difficulty in assessing the quality of software and still more in assessing its suitability for a particular business. It is because of this that the professional competence of the supplier is particularly important.

If consultants are not to assist in supplier selection, an initial list of possible suppliers may be obtained from telephone and professional directories, and publications such as the Computer Users Year Book. A first telephone call to a supplier should seek to establish that he offers local software and hardware support and has other customers in a similar type of business. With information from these customers or other contacts it should be possible to reach a short list of say five suppliers. Each should then be provided with information from the requirements statement (description of the business, applications envisaged and volumes) and invited to an initial discussion.

At these discussions it should be possible to obtain much useful information and it is likely that, as a result, additions or modifications could be made to the requirements statement. It is important, however, to avoid pure sales talk and always to turn the conversation back to the system required and to the software facilities available for these systems. Every effort should be made even at this stage to note the exact response of suppliers to the points detailed in Appendix A, the type of equipment they would offer and to elicit from them what steps they would want to take before making a quotation.

Call for proposals

Following these discussions it should be possible to select two or perhaps three suppliers to make proposals. They should be asked to include:

1 Application packages and software utilities (see glossary) to be supplied and the prices;
2 Technical details of the hardware and unit prices;
3 List of all other costs which will be involved in the installation including appropriate systems analysis, program package modifications, wiring costs for distant terminals and user training;
4 Details of hardware and software maintenance services and costs;
5 Statement of ability to provide satisfactory working systems, including as a minimum the reports, facilities and all information fields for main files as given in the requirements statement;
6 Estimates of systems usage for each application based on the volumes of data given, particularly in relation to any peak periods;
7 A description of how the equipment can be upgraded for additional applications or extra volumes of work;
8 Details of support (advice, training, etc.) for initial installation and subsequently.

Suppliers at this stage will need to be provided with the full requirements statement, revised as necessary following discussions with the various suppliers. They should also be provided with any relevant information they may request particularly to clarify any involved rules, for example, for pricing customer invoices. The list of fields held in main files may suitably be used as a check list to ensure that all requirements are understood. It is undoubtedly advisable to give suppliers as much assistance as possible at this stage, remembering that they have to offset their costs against the possibility of a sale and that their sales margins for equipment valued at up to £10,000 are not large.

The proposals received should be evaluated in the light of the information provided in Appendix A. All aspects are important but the key aspects are worth emphasis:

1 If possible a supplier who takes overall responsibility for all aspects;
2 Supplier's reputation in the particular applications;
3 Good documentation and support.

In regard to the last point it is reasonable for each of the initial applications to request a copy of the systems documentation which the supplier issues to users. Although it will be impossible to check all points, it should be possible to assess its quality by examining a few.

Another aspect for early attention with all but the smallest systems is the supplier's standard form of contract. The wise purchaser will seek to negotiate points of difficulty in these contracts and will start to do this well before the time arises for signing the contract. Once the supplier senses that he is likely to receive the order, he may be less willing to vary a standard contract.

9

Going
Ahead

The basic choice

On calling for proposals from suppliers an important decision has to
be made on the level of computing involvement the owner or
manager of the business is prepared to undertake personally. If the
owner is looking for a turn-key system with full responsibility for
maintenance, training and support being provided by the supplier,
then the systems/software house is likely to be the best choice and
the remaining sections of this chapter are directly relevant. If
however, in view of the scale of the project, the owner is prepared to
do most of the installation himself and is also prepared, if necessary,
to undertake fault finding and program amendment, a system
provided by a local dealer may be appropriate. The standard of
support will be less than most business men would require but the
initial cost will certainly be less. In such circumstances the purchaser
should not be too insistent upon the dealer meeting the criteria
given in this chapter, as many dealers will simply be unable to do so.

Plan and budget

On receipt of proposals from competing suppliers, enough information will be available to draw up a plan showing the various actions
to be taken to set up first the installation and then each application.
For the installation itself, the plan will include the provision of space
and electric power. For each application the plan will include any
modification of input documents, agreed operating methods, systems testing, file creation and parallel running.

The plan should be kept as simple as possible. It should be divided into stages and adequate time should be allowed for each stage. Staff who know the detail of present methods of working and other staff who may be affected by the introduction of the computer need to be informed of the plan and their comments should be sought. There may be fears regarding the future – some justified, some not justified – and it is important that these should be openly discussed. The object is to ensure that the plan is sensibly based and that there are no mental blockages so that, when the decision is taken to go ahead, there will be no unforeseen problems. If problems are revealed at this stage then it may be perfectly proper to delay going ahead or even to abandon the project until circumstances have changed.

Though a full list of actions has been compiled and a due time allowance given to each, the overall time will probably be longer than initially thought likely. If file set-up is unusually large it may be necessary to obtain outside assistance. In any event, an approximate estimate of costs for these various actions should be made. From this and from the checklist of costs given in Appendix A, total set-up costs and monthly running costs should be estimated. These costs compared with any alternative methods and with the benefits expected will indicate whether the project should be pursued. If changes of business method and/or special programming are involved, the financial case needs to be good, for while there are likely to be additional benefits which cannot be quantified (e.g. better information), there may also be unforeseen problems and hence additional costs.

Negotiate the contract

Once all the work of specifying requirements and of selecting a supplier has been completed there is a natural temptation to sign without demur the standard contract which the salesman will offer. This should not be done.

There are good reasons for examining closely the small print on any commercial contract and there are special reasons for exercising caution with computer contracts. Standard contracts are naturally framed to protect the supplier's rather than the client's interests. Some points may require negotiation and if negotiations are to be effective they should be undertaken while the supplier is still competing for the business. During negotiations it should be remembered that a good contract is not to be regarded primarily as a basis for legal action but it should envisage possible problems, provide for solutions and hence help to avoid disputes.

The wording of standard forms of contract is not sacrosanct. Alterations can be made in ordinary handwriting on the text itself or be effected by an accompanying letter. In some circumstances the supplier may agree to complete re-typing. It is unlikely, however, that a supplier will be prepared to make more than limited alterations in order to secure an order from a small business. Alterations will probably have to be referred to the supplier's head office and the local salesman will earn no kudos for it. None-the-less the user should be aware of two problems which arise in standard contracts.

Firstly, standard contracts for hardware and software are usually separate documents, the hardware taking the form of a contract of sale (or rental) and the software being a licence to use. From the user's point of view, however, the hardware is useless without good software and the software is useless if there are hardware failures. The user is in fact interested in the system as a whole; he wants to know that hardware and software together will meet his requirements and that the supplier will work together with him until the systems are fully operational. The final form of contract ought to reflect this need.

Secondly, standard contracts, once signed, will generally in law constitute the total agreement between parties. Verbal undertakings by the salesman and even written systems proposals made by the suppliers may be valueless in a dispute unless they are specifically referred to in the contracts.

In order to overcome these two problems and to secure a satisfactory contract the user should:

1   Negotiate a written agreement to link the various standard contracts and to incorporate a warranty that the system will perform as represented in the sales proposal, the requirements statement and as agreed in any other specified documents;

2   Negotiate for appropriate dates of payment;

3   Examine the standard contracts for exclusions and other clauses

which might reduce the supplier's responsibilities in any substantial matter;

4   Have the contracts checked by his solicitor.

In practical terms the dates of payment are particularly important in securing the client's needs. While a 10% payment may be required with the hardware and software order, the balance of both the hardware and software should not be required until all the hardware has been delivered and the software, for the first application, has been operating satisfactorily over a period of at least a week, preferably a month.

Install, set up and train

Installation of the computer itself will be carried out by the supplier. The user has to prepare a suitable room or space for the equipment (see Chapter 10).

In most business applications, master files of information will have to be set up on disk before operations can commence. For a small file this could probably be done in one or two hours but for a large file of customers or stock items the work might extend over some weeks.

The stages are:

1   Sorting and checking the written documents from which the file is to be created;
2   Addition of codes (defining or classifying customers or products etc.) which are to be used in the computer system;
3   Keying this information and input to the computer;
4   Computer printing the file for visual check followed as necessary by the input of amendments.

The input of actual balances on each account may be left until immediately before the system is made operational. Detailed instructions for the way the data and balances are to be input will be contained in the user's manual which is supplied with the application software.

It may be found that some of the documents to be used when keying in to the computer are not well suited to the purpose. The relevant information may not appear in the same place on every document, the sequence of information may be unsatisfactory or the information may not be directly available to the operator but require deduction from other data. It is very important to avoid errors at input and it may well be that some document re-design or some change in the method by which the input document is completed will be required.

For accounting applications it will be particularly necessary to consider jointly with the auditors the form of control accounts which are to be used and to set these up. The auditors will also wish to be consulted regarding the form of audit trail offered by the package.

The general method of operating computers of the type described in this book can be learnt in under a day. Learning how to operate an application package, in other words understanding the various forms of input, the facilities available, the error correction procedures, and so on, will normally take substantially longer. Operator training is normally carried out on site by the supplier as part of the initial testing of the application. Some suppliers augment this with more formal two-day courses so that all facilities are well understood.

Training in the general use of the computer and training in its use for any particular application are not, of course, to be confused with programmer training. The nature of programming and some indication of the training required were given in Chapter 3.

Parallel run, go operational

The last stage of preparation is the parallel run. A parallel run is simply the operation of the computer on current data and exactly as required for operational work but in parallel with the existing manual or mechanical system. The output from the two systems is then compared over a period of possibly two weeks or perhaps as much as two months. If there are misunderstandings of system requirements, or if errors exist in the software they will then probably be detected. If there are faults which cannot be quickly corrected, it is possible to fall back on the manual system.

Parallel running requires additional effort and is sometimes difficult to organise. Very experienced teams sometimes take the gamble of avoiding it, but if they do so, they plan, check and test very thoroughly before the transfer. For companies installing their first application a period of parallel running should be regarded as essential.

Generally speaking, a new application is parallel run complete and taken over complete. There are two possible exceptions to this. The first is when the master file and all the processing is easily handled in sections. This could apply in a stock control application. One section of stock only could be parallel run and when the software has been thoroughly proved, other sections might be progressively transferred without a prallel run. The second exception to the complete parallel run is an account by account take over. In some types of applications (e.g. insurance broking policy renewals) where the account typically moves only a few times each year, it is possible to take accounts on to the computer system at the time when they move. In such a situation, after an initial parallel run on relatively few accounts, the take-over proceeds gradually month-by-month until the work is entirely transferred. The benefits of the full computer system are delayed but the risks in changeover are minimised.

10

Successful Computer Operations

The importance of reliability

The most important aspects of a business computer system are its suitability for the business and its reliability. Much has been said about suitability in the chapter on selection. Reliability requires continuing support from a good supplier together with the adoption of sound operating practices on the part of the user. This chapter considers possible causes of operational failure and how, by following good practices, these failures can be avoided or their effects minimised.

The computer environment

Small computers will operate in normal office conditions and there should be no difficulty in meeting temperature and humidity requirements. It is important to avoid dust, for dust particles on floppy disks can corrupt data recording/reading. Protection against possible variations in the electrical supply which can corrupt data in course of being processed can be obtained by installing a voltage stabiliser. It is necessary to take precautions against fire, theft and, what is perhaps more likely, improper tampering with the equipment. Thus access to the room or area occupied by the computer should be restricted to those authorised to use it. When not in use the room should be locked and there may also be a lock on the computer itself. There should be a lockable, fireproof cupboard for the storage of disks. The disks themselves may have little value, but loss of the information held on them could be crippling.

Hardware maintenance

The electronic circuitry of modern computers will function for long periods fault-free. Components which contain moving mechanical parts (e.g. the printer and disk drives) are less reliable. Regular preventive maintenance for the mechanical parts and a fast response to failure in the computer as a whole are necessary.

The standard of maintenance is dependant upon the supplier of the computing equipment.

The quality of maintenance provided by the local dealer is likely to be variable depending on his resources. Thus, response times to a fault may vary from one day to six weeks. The best method of determining the quality of maintenance provided by an individual dealer is to talk to existing customers.

The situation is different with equipment supplied directly by original equipment manufacturers or systems houses. They will provide regular preventive maintenance and a fast response to any failure of the computer.

Many original equipment manufacturers provide hardware maintenance through their own service organisation but, unless they support a large local market, their engineering centre may be distant. An alternative is to use one of the companies who specialise in providing a contract maintenance service. Since their livelihood depends on providing maintenance rather than selling equipment there is possibly more pressure on them to provide good support. In any event it is desirable to arrange the contract through the suppliers in order to maintain their overall responsibility for both hardware and software.

The possibility of using back-up equipment should not be overlooked. As hardware costs are now relatively low, the supplier may actually hold back-up equipment which can be used in an emergency, or it may seem worthwhile for the user himself to hold, say, a spare disk drive. Another possibility is an agreement with a neighbouring firm who has similar equipment for a back-up service. In making decisions of this type, the user will need to consider how important his computer applications are in the running of his business and how long he can afford to be without his computer.

Software and system support

As with hardware support, a clear distinction must be made between software obtained through local dealers and that obtained from systems houses or original equipment manufacturers.

Local dealers
The quality of software support varies from negligible to excellent, depending upon local staff resources. The usual standard is that simple enquiries can normally be dealt with locally but more complex problems will be referred to the original supplier of the software package. This may cause considerable inconvenience.

Systems houses and software houses
Software support provided under a maintenance agreement can be at two levels:

1   The provision of immediate assistance over the telephone for problems caused by operator error or misunderstanding of documentation;
2   Assistance with more serious problems caused by program errors (these may be rectified by the software house logging into the client's computer via the telephone system and an acoustic coupler and correcting the fault directly, or alternatively, by a site visit of a software specialist).

Data security

As computer systems develop, files of information which were formerly held in written records will be progressively transferred to disk storage. Complete loss of this information could be a severe impediment to the running of the business and its reconstitution would probably take some months and in any event be very costly. The risks to this information should therefore be understood. Files kept on disk can sometimes be accidently overwritten by the computer thereby destroying information. Floppy disks are delicate and mishandling is likely to cause information loss. Writing across a disk with a biro, even if the disk is in its protective jacket, will destroy information. An upset cup of coffee can render a disk useless.

Protection against such disasters should be provided by the copying of disk files at regular intervals (floppy to floppy; hard disk to tape cartridge or floppy). The copies should be stored in a fireproof cabinet or possibly with the bank. If then, for example, weekly copies are made and the current data file is accidentally destroyed, at worst only one week's transactions will have to be re-entered. It is also helpful regularly to produce printed reports which are filed in a conventional filing cabinet. Such reports together with appropriate copy invoices or other usual paperwork will allow reconstruction of files should disaster occur.

There is risk that data files may be corrupted for fraudulent purposes. In a small business, however, the risk of fraud should not be great, because directors are likely to be closely in touch with what is going on. The auditors also will require information to be provided from the files (the audit trail) so that they can apply the necessary checks.

If the directors consider that some part of the information or system (e.g. payments to staff) should not be known to the normal operators, they will have to appoint a person to run that particular system. If the information is held on floppy disks, these disks will have to be kept in a separate locked cabinet. Some systems prevent access to particular programs and data files unless a password is input. This is known as password protection. If hard disks are installed they are permanently on line and password protection for confidential information is essential. The password, as its name implies, is a code known only to each authorised person. Any attempt to access information or programs which are password protected will be rejected by the computer unless the password is quoted.

Note that in the UK and some other countries computer storage of personal information is subject to legal requirements being met. Such legislation is designed to protect the individual against the misuse or unauthorised disclosure of computerised data, and to ensure that personal data files are accurate and kept up to date.

Operating discipline

The need for operating discipline will already have become clear from the preceding paragraphs. With a well run computer system

there will be a set of standing instructions to be followed and these
will include:

1 Actions/checks at switch 'on' and 'off';
2 Daily schedules of work to be done;
3 Filing of diskettes;
4 Daily, weekly and other copying of disk files;
5 Creation and filing of print-outs for control and audit;
6 Checks to be made on system failure before calling for service
   (e.g. connections, switches, floppies correctly inserted, etc.);
7 Maintenance of fault log – date, time, fault observed, action
   taken, engineer or other response;
8 Action in the event of fire.

If operating discipline is to be maintained there will be a need to
train new staff and to ensure if at all possible that when staff leave
they hand over correctly. The standing instructions, provided they
are kept up-to-date, will be invaluable in this respect. The responsibility of the manager in regard to this is obvious.

Changes of system and documentation

The documentation supplied with each application program falls
into two parts:

1 Operating section providing instructions for running and how to
   respond to emergency situations;
2 Controls manual providing a description of the application, its
   validity tests and its control procedures.

This documentation is an important record and should be treated
as such. Auditors may well want to refer to it. It is valuable in the
education of new employees and, if a need arises to change the
system, reference to it will be essential.

It is sometimes said that computer systems are rigid and inhibit
change. There is a large element of truth in this but it is not the
whole truth. A computer system is best viewed as a framework.
Changes within the framework can normally be made easily but a
change outside the framework is likely to be difficult. The
framework itself consists of the files and the main program(s) but
good programs usually offer the user a number of options.

The user can readily change from one option to another and he will also be able to vary the contents of tables, for example price rates. These are changes within the framework and are easily handled, provided there is a clear understanding of what is involved and a definite date on which the change is to be made. Additional reports or changes in reports, which do not require changes in file layouts, can easily be provided. More extensive changes call for significant program alterations. These require planning, time for re-programming and testing and are inevitably expensive.

The systems documentation is the base information from which the way to plan any change in an application must be made. Thus it is essential that the documentation should be well kept and that it is updated with changes as they are made. It is in the nature of the business to change and it is good practice, while questioning the reasons for change, to be able to make changes smoothly when they are necessary.

The above warnings over the difficulties of changing the system are much less severe when applied to systems based on information retrieval packages, since these systems normally cater for a degree of redesign. However, a new difficulty can arise, particularly when the systems are 'programmed' by the user – namely the lack of documentation. It can be extremely difficult to reprogram a system that was originally designed a year or more ago if there are no notes available on the system design.

11

Word Processing

Nature of word processing

Word processing is the preparation of typescript, using computing facilities for the storage and manipulation of text. The techniques differ in many respects from those of data processing. Word processing does not follow the formal data structures (file/record/field) of data processing and the typist using a word processor has a very different job from the operator of a computer terminal or, indeed, from that of a normal typist.

A small business having a need for word processing could either install a dedicated word processor or acquire a word processing package for use on a microcomputer. A word processor is similar to the business computer described in Chapter 4; like the stand alone machine it has a keyboard, a screen, two disk drives and a printer. When text is keyed in by the typist, it is displayed on the screen and may be stored on disk. At any time the stored text may be amended or printed. The essential difference from the typewriter is that printing is not the direct result of keying but is a transfer of data from the store.

When several operators require facilities, a shared resource machine supporting several keyboards and screens may be used. A high quality printer (generally daisy wheel) is used with word processors and is normal with a computer on which word processing is installed as a package.

As a general rule, if word processing is the major requirement for a microcomputer system a dedicated word processing system is much simpler to use than an equivalent program package on a microcomputer.

Uses of word processing

The advantage of a word processor compared with a typewriter is an improvement in typist productivity. Facilities which help to provide this gain are:

1　Fast set up of line width, tabulation settings, page size, and so on;
2　Ability to correct typing errors before printing;
3　Ability to print final typescript from a draft prepared on the processor by simply entering the amendments rather than by retyping the whole (this also avoids the entry of new errors on the second typing);
4　General ability to call up from disk storage any text, lists, standard paragraphs, names and addresses, and so on, which have been recorded there and then to amend and print these as required;
5　Ability to merge name and address lists with standard text to produce personalised letters.

Typical applications with a broad indication of possible savings of typing time are:

		Typist time reduced by
1	Retyping of manuals, contracts, standing instructions etc. with little change	75%
2	Typing of letters of which 90% are standard paragraphs	75%
3	Retyping of price lists, directories etc. with 15% revision	50%
4	Typing of a draft report followed by one revision	45%

If the original of any document is prepared by word processor a small number of copies may, of course, be printed on the machine but when a large number of copies is required offset litho is likely to be cheaper. For technical manuals the processor is particularly valuable both for preparing the original document and for updating it in response to changes. With a high quality printer the preparation of camera-ready copy for lithography is easy.

Considerations in regard to use

The saving in typing time which is possible with a word processor depends on the repetitive element in the typing. If there is no repetition there can be little or no benefit when compared with a normal typewriter. Thus in judging whether or not to use a word processor an analysis of the typing load is required, but this has to be related back to the proportion of each typist's time which is actually spent in typing. In a small business the typists usually have many duties other than typing. Thus a 75% reduction in typing time on half the typing load would give a 38% saving over the full load; but if typing occupied only half the typist's day, the saving of typist's time would be only 19%.

Before deciding to install a word processor it is necessary to consider the abilities of the typists. Experience has shown that word processing techniques are successfully implemented only when there is at least one highly motivated secretary to pioneer their use. This person has to devote a considerable amount of time in ultimately mastering the complexities of the operating instructions – typically up to 200 A4 pages of text. However, this is not as daunting as it may first seem to appear, as a shortened (condensed) version of the operating instructions, one or two A4 pages, will enable limited operation whilst expertise is gained. The secretary should, when possible, be sent on a short training course and subsequently be able to obtain technical advice in regard to implementing new procedures. Thereafter daily use of the word processor is desirable. Without it the problem of recalling the appropriate instructions for each operation is such that most typists would probably prefer to carry out the work on an ordinary typewriter. The work should also be understood and practised by a second typist so that for those office procedures which depend on word processing, there will be cover for sickness, holidays or resignation. A useful partial safeguard is to insist that a manual of standard procedures is prepared by the operator as procedures are developed. This will minutely detail the way each task is carried out.

In broad terms the facilities and problems of word processor use apply also to word processing packages installed on microcomputers. It is generally agreed that word processors can be attractive in professional offices (e.g. solicitors), where there is a large and suitable work load. The package alternative with its lower cost (the computer presumably having been justified on other grounds) may be attractive for certain specific and limited tasks. An example of this is given under Case Studies – ABB Ltd. When there is a choice – as there is for a mailing list – between the word processor or the data processing method the more structured approach of data processing will be easier for the operator to follow.

Checklist

Software characteristics

* Does it have good editing facilities, working on a facsimile of the text as it would appear on paper?

* Is it easy to correct, insert, delete, append, centre and underline text instantly, indicating the outcome of each operation by adjusting the appearance of the screen?

* Is it easy to set up a standard letter format?

* Will it automatically control line length doing either left justification, right justification or justifying both margins on demand?

* Are the ends of paragraphs protected by a special command?

* Can it produce an index?

* Is it easy to set and clear tabulations? (Does one have to set tabs at the start?)

* Is there a character scale on the VDU which will allow easy manual tabulation?

* Can one back-space over a tab setting to permit the typing of uneven length columns?

* Does it have back-space control to put additional characters above existing characters, e.g. u and ¨ to give ü?

* Is it possible to underscore along a whole set line containing no text?

* Are margins easy to set? When set, is automatic continuous typing possible without using the return key?

* Are indented margins (multiple or not) easy to set up and remove?

* Is it possible to split words between lines? In other words, does it have a soft hyphenation facility?

* Is it possible to insert a new column into an existing table and remove columns later?

* Is there automatic page throw?

* Will it do subscripts and superscripts?

  } where applicable

* Will it do scientific symbols?

* Are 'widow lines' held?

* Is page numbering adjusted when text is removed?

* Does tabulation or the use of sub- and superscripts invalidate character and line counting?

* Can address list and name file be merged with a standard letter to produce a set of personalised standard letters?

* Is it easy to prepare documents by merging standard blocks of text taken from file?

* Will it automatically number pages?

* How quickly can one move from page 1 to page 6 say, and back?

* Is there the facility to insert additional chapters in a document already in existence and already numbered?

* Is it simple to check existing text controls and remove or alter them?

* Is it simple to remove existing text controls?

VDU and computer
* Is the display suitable for long periods of continuous use? Can the brightness be adjusted?

* Is the feel of the keyboard acceptable to the professional typist?

* How many lines can be simultaneously displayed on the screen?

* How many characters per line? (A minimum of 80 characters/ line.)

* How many characters of the text can be stored in the computer memory? (An A4 page of single spacing contains about 3,000 characters of text.)

* Which keys are adjacent to the shift keys? (Accidental striking of adjacent keys may have unfortunate results.)

Disk drives and disks
* How many characters of text can be stored on a single disk?

* Are the disks hard disks or floppy disks? (Hard disks have greater capacity than floppy disks and are very much more reliable, they are also more expensive.)

* Does the system have dual disk drives?

* Is the system expandable?

Printer
* Is the print quality acceptable?

* Is there a choice of pitch?

* Is the printer speed acceptable?

* Will the printer accept continuous stationery in various widths?

* Is there a tractor feed mechanism for precise registration, necessary for the printing of labels?

* Will the printer accept single sheet paper fed by hand?

* Is a hopper available so that single sheets may be fed automatically and reliably?

* Is there a wide choice of typeface?

* How easy is it to change from one typeface to another during the course of printing?

* How easy is it to change paper?

* How easy is it to change ribbons?

* What is the life expectancy of the print head?

* Are both one-strike and multi-strike ribbons available?

* What is the cost of both types of ribbons?

* Are supplies of stationery, print heads, and ribbons readily available from suppliers of computer products other than the manufacturer of the printer?

* Is the printer noisy?

* Can the printer copy with subscript and superscript and maintain alignment of the print? (This latter point is most important.)

Hardware service
* What is the cost of hardware maintenance?

* What items are covered in the maintenance contract?

* Does the contract include parts, labour and travelling expenses?

* What is the response time from the report of the fault to the time an engineer attends?

* Is the maintenance done on site?

* If the fault cannot be rectified on site is a replacement unit provided?

* Is there a local maintenance organisation?

* Do the suppliers carry out their own maintenance or employ a specialist maintenance company?

* If a specialist company, have you seen their conditions of business?

* What is the local availability of spare parts?

* Are the supplier and the manufacturer sufficiently well established so that one may be reasonably sure they will still be trading in the UK in five years time?

* Have you checked with users of similar machines in order to verify the quality of the hardware and support?

Operator training

* Is the operation of the word processor clearly described and explained in the manual provided? Is the explanation readily understandable to the beginner?

* Does the supplier provide adequate training for your staff?

* What is the cost of training?

* Does the supplier provide an enquiry service for difficult operations? (Is there a charge for this service?)

* Is training given on site, locally or only in major cities?

* Can your own staff communicate their skills to colleagues once they have been acquired?

Final question

Have you a secretary who is sufficiently motivated to work through the considerable difficulties involved in the implementation of a word processor?

Case Studies

These six case studies were selected on the basis that the business should be small and the capital value of the computer installation should not exceed £12,000. They do not necessarily constitute a representative cross section of such installations, but do give some indication of what one may expect. Five of the six studies are of installations which have probably had more than average success. The type of problems experienced by the sixth (AEE Ltd) have persisted far longer in some companies.

The titles of the six companies are of course imaginary and information has not been provided which would clearly indicate the suppliers or manufacturers. In other respects the information given is factual so that it provides a reasonable picture of computing costs, problems and benefits.

The following points may be helpful:

1   Five of the six companies found suppliers who took overall responsibility for hardware and software whereas the sixth started on the premise that a manager would write the programs;
2   Directors/senior managers were actively involved in the development of systems at five of the six companies. In the sixth (AEE Ltd) the director controlled the situation in a broad managerial sense only;
3   Despite their active involvement directors at three companies had no knowledge of programming – nor had any member of their staffs;
4   Computer memory sizes are given as a guide but this is not

absolute evidence of available memory and is not directly related to computing power;
5   Today's prices are probably *less* than the 1980/1 prices quoted in this section.

AAA Ltd

The company
AAA Ltd is a firm of printers employing seventeen staff and with an annual turnover of £300,000. All the business is conducted from one site.

The applications
Sales ledger. (350 accounts. 600 transactions per month. Open item method)
Purchase ledger. (120 accounts. 100 transactions per month)
Nominal ledger. (70 accounts integrated with sales and purchase ledgers)
Payroll.

The computer
CPU of 32K bytes with one VDU, 150 cps printer and 3 floppy disk drives.
Capital cost: £8,000 (1980) and maintenance £800 p.a.
Software supplied by hardware supplier.
Capital cost £2,000.
No maintenance contract but software faults corrected by supplier free of charge.

How supplier selected
A bureau service had been used for some years. There had been personal contact with the suppliers of the in-house system over several years. They were known to offer good support for accounting applications and they offered a system programmed in BASIC (see below).

Training and time scale
The managing director had previously acquired skill as a hobbyist using BASIC and he took two days training in the use of the

packages. The supplier's representative sat in for one week with the operator. The feasibility of setting up an in-house system to take over the bureau work was considered over a period of some nine months, installation was achieved one month from order and the first application was running two weeks later. In this last period there was intensive effort by the managing director and throughout there was good cooperation from the supplier.

Problems

1. Programs for sales ledger and purchase ledger, written apparently by different programmers, had different conventions from the operator's viewpoint. These were reduced by program changes (later versions said to have had this corrected);
2. Cash allocation required program changes to accord with management requirements;
3. Some floppy disks had unsatisfactory coating and extensive re-running was required to reconstitute records.

Benefits realised

Bureau services were replaced at little extra cost. As against the bureau there were marked advantages in being able to retain all documents in the office and from the provision of enquiry facilities on ledger accounts. The computer system has provided better checks on cash flow and profitability assessment than former clerical methods.

Further plans

The sales ledger systems may be extended to order and invoicing procedures, but the method of pricing sales does not lend itself to full mechanisation.

ABB Ltd

The company

ABB Ltd is a firm of insurance brokers, handling general insurance but with the emphasis on commercial and industrial risks. They employ five staff and have a total premium income of £1m p.a. All business is conducted from one site.

The application

Preparation of renewal notices. (2,500 notices p.a.)

Clients' ledgers. (400 accounts, 3,500 transactions p.a.)

Analysis of brokerage charged and payments due to insurance companies.

Word processing. (planned)

The computer

CPU of 16K bytes with 1 VDU, 1 daisy wheel printer and 2 floppy disk drives.

Capital cost £9,000 (1980). Maintenance £900 p.a.

Software supplied by software house £3,000 plus word processing £1,500.

Maintenance contract for software at nominal annual charge plus hourly rate.

Faults corrected by supplier during first 30 days free of charge.

How supplier selected

Another broker recommended the hardware supplier, and the hardware supplier recommended the software house. The software house had written programs for an insurance broker to be run on similar equipment but using hard disks. Some changes were made to the software, but no firm undertaking was given that faults would not arise because of the different types of disks. Programs were written in BASIC.

Training and time scale

ABB Ltd was formed following the reorganisation of a larger group and had to set up its own accounting system at short notice. The directors had a background knowledge of machine accounting but no previous experience of computing. Hardware was installed in late 1980 and the software house gave on-site instruction for one day. Operating instructions and the menu approach were found easy to follow.

Problems

1   A serial number is automatically allocated to every transaction by the software. At some point there was a duplication of serial numbers leading to wrong postings to clients' accounts;

2   Miscellaneous minor difficulties said to be due to the adaptation of the original software for floppy disk working;
3   Clients' accounts having many transactions could not be fully displayed on the screen. This was software limitation apparently due to a difference in the requirements of this client's business from those for which the software was originally written;
4   The software house is sixty miles distant and this results in high telephone charges for checking out queries;
5   The accountants have complained of inadequate controls and audit trail.

Benefits realised
Four months after installation the transfer of clients' records was continuing as planned but it was too early to assume that further program faults would not appear. Additional business was envisaged, without extra staff, and it seemed probable that the aims of the installation would be achieved.

Further plans
Word processing is to be developed primarily to keep updated records of clients' policies. If business continues to expand the floppy disks will be changed to hard disk drives.

ACC Ltd

The company
ACC Ltd is a retailer selling high quality furniture and furnishings most of which it imports. There are 25 staff and a turnover of £1m p.a. All the business is conducted from one site but the customers are widespread.

The applications
Purchase ledger. (450 accounts. 1,500 transactions per month)
Nominal ledger. (75 accounts, integral with purchase ledger)
Balance forward method used.

The computer
CPU 32K bytes with 1 VDU, 150 cps printer and 3 floppy disk drives.

Capital cost £8,000 (1980). Maintenance £800 per annum.
Software supplied by hardware supplier. Capital cost £1,000.
No maintenance charge but software faults corrected free of charge.

How supplier selected
The supplier was well known to the directors and had installed similar systems previously.

Training and time scale
No member of staff had previous computer experience. A one day course was provided and the supplier's representative gave 'hands on' instruction for one week full time and some seven days at odd times thereafter. After three months, during which time there were a number of telephone calls for advice, the staff concerned felt fully competent.

Problems
1 Hardware fault led to faulty information on disk. Although the fault was corrected, much effort was required to correct the data;
2 The software coped with VAT on imports but was not well suited to this requirement.

Benefits realised
The need to replace a clerk who left was avoided. The system helps in assessing quantity discounts which are allowed on yearly take-offs. The computer system is less prone to error than the manual system by reason of the integration of the purchase and nominal ledger systems.

Further plans
Payroll will be added in due course.

ADD Ltd

The company
ADD Ltd makes jam and employs some 100 staff in production, distribution and marketing. There is one factory and a separate

warehouse for despatch of packed stock. A small computer is used for accounting applications. This case study, however, is solely concerned with a computer used for production records.

The application
Production records. Production planning depends on sales forecasts, on the assembly of raw materials, containers and packings, and on recipes (sugar, pectin, etc.) which depend on the quality of the fruit. There is one manufacturing line which is switched between fifteen types of fruit, each type being packed in fifteen different ways.

The computer produces daily statistics of material usages, product makes, losses and quantities warehoused, with records of lot numbers to check against complaints, etc. Fruit quality/origin and recipes for each production run are also recorded to provide experience data for future quality control. Information is summarised for each week and cumulatively for the year. At year end two 5-inch floppies hold all the information by days of production and a further two hold similar information by product.

The computer
CPU of 32K bytes, with 1 VDU, an 80 column printer and 2 floppy disk drives. Capital cost £1,850 (1983).

How supplier selected
The manager responsible for production planning, based on limited experience as described below, selected low-cost hardware which was easy to program in BASIC. He planned to develop all programs himself.

Training and time scale
The manager had previously acquired experience at a one day informal course plus about 50 hours BASIC programming and experiment on a machine which he was able to use at home in his spare time. Production records were then maintained by a clerk but in 1979 the clerk resigned and was not replaced. Recording was cut to a minimum but proved intractable and the computer was sanctioned for the personal use of the manager. The input programs

were written by him largely in his spare time over a period of two months.

Problems
There have been no significant hardware faults during the first year's operation. Reprogramming for errors and for changes of requirements has been done by the manager.

Benefits realised
There is a clerical saving as described above. More important is the ability to analyse current production problems by rapid reference to previous records. This is done more quickly and efficiently than was previously possible and is of major assistance in rapidly correcting variations from normal production standards.

AEE Ltd

The company
AEE Ltd is a wholesaler of carnival and other paper goods, marketing some 400 lines. Goods are received from over twenty manufacturing units and distributed countrywide from one central warehouse.

The application
Sales invoicing and sales ledger (800 accounts, 600 transactions per month). Purchase planning. A forward plan is needed because of the variability of demand, the heavy Christmas peak and the scope for selecting suppliers in relation to required delivery dates, and so on.

The computer
CPU of 48K bytes with 1 VDU, an 80 column printer and 2 floppy disk drives. Capital cost £3,500 (1981). Sales invoicing and sales ledger software including modifications £1,000. Hardware maintenance £350 p.a.

How supplier selected
The director responsible was at first primarily interested in purchase

planning but after various discussions over some 18 months considered that it would be simpler to start on invoicing and sales ledger. He selected a make of computer based on price and general reputation and found a local supplier who would also take responsibility for software.

Training and time scale
No member of staff had previous computer experience and no list of requirements was drawn up. After a half-day's examination by one of the supplier's team a software package for invoicing and sales ledger was selected but it was recognised that some modifications would be required. In order to establish the exact requirements the supplier demonstrated the package over a two day period to the director and the chief clerk but (not altogether surprisingly) they failed to perceive all the differences between the package and what they wanted.

Problems
Shortly before the computer was delivered, the supplier's representative who had examined requirements left the company, which upset the installation plans. Very soon after installation an intermittent fault occurred (eventually diagnosed as a cold joint on the main computer board) but it was two weeks before it was clearly recognised. A component was then replaced but intermittent faults continued. Eight weeks after delivery the machine was replaced.

As a result of trials during the eight weeks it became clear that the software did not meet the user's requirements as follows:

1 No consignee could be shown on invoices;
2 Certain fields (e.g. invoicee's reference number) were not large enough;
3 Fractions of normal standard lot sizes (used only occasionally) could not be handled;
4 VAT not shown separately on statements. VAT was correctly calculated on invoiced amount less cash discount but on receiving their statements the customers deducted cash discount from the one total figure, in other words, they underpaid.

Benefits realised
Ten weeks after the original computer was delivered no useful

results had been achieved. Trials of the new machine awaited further modification of the software. Due to the structure of the programs in the original package there will probably have to be some compromise between what is desired and what is possible but the supplier intends to provide a sound system. Given this, the client will cease using his present accounting machine and should have better facilities for little extra cost.

Further plans
These depend on success with the sales ledger but purchase planning will be attempted using VisiCalc – see Chapter 3.

AFF Ltd

The company
AFF Ltd is a builders merchants employing some 35 staff and handling around 10,000 stock lines.

The applications
Sales ledger. (1,200 accounts, 3,200 transactions per month)
Purchase ledger. (160 accounts, 600 transactions per month)
Nominal ledger. (80 accounts, transactions integrated with purchases)
Payroll. (50 staff weekly – includes an associated company)
Open item method used.

The computer
CPU of 64K bytes with 1 VDU, 120 cps printer, 3 floppy disk drives. Capital cost £6,600 (1980), software cost £2,000, hardware maintenance £800 p.a. Cost of folders, stationery stand and initial stationery stocks £1,500.

How supplier selected
The managing director visited business exhibitions for several years and discussed his problems with various suppliers. Considered use of a bureau but found that in-house computer would be cheaper. Selected a supplier who was personally recommended, whose offices were not more than 20 miles distant and who undertook responsibility for hardware and software.

Training and time scale

There was a period of about ten months in which the scope of the project was determined prior to placing an order. One month later the equipment was delivered and there was then some two months parallel running before the first application was fully operational. A second director was at this stage nominated to take charge of the operation. The senior operator who had considerable experience of accounting machines was given a three day training course and three other staff who sometimes operate the computer acquired sufficient skills in about two weeks. The fourth application (payroll) was brought into operation six months after the first.

Problems

1 Only two minor modifications were needed to the standard software;
2 There have been no real problems apart from read/write failures with some floppy disks;
3 A constraint arises from floppy disk on-line storage capacity which requires the sales ledger to be processed as four sections, one section per floppy disk.

Benefits realised

Workloads have increased without a need for extra staff. Sundry debtors have been reduced from an average of £165,000 to £125,000 due to timely statements and follow up action on aged debtor analysis. The business is under better control.

Further plans

Stock control is envisaged once a full experience of present applications has been gained. It is recognised that this will demand systems study and upgrading of the equipment.

Appendix A

Checklists

The supplier

* Is the supplier taking overall responsibility for both software and hardware installation and performance? A supplier who accepts overall responsibility will be more careful in his specification of hardware and software than one who has only a partial responsibility. It is disastrous to be in the no-man's-land between two suppliers, when the cause of a fault is uncertain.

* How many computer systems has he installed in the last three years? (Is he well established and likely to be able to provide continuing service?)

* What experience has the supplier generally, and his local staff in particular, in your type of business?

* How many programmers has he and, if you are in difficulties, from what office will your immediate support come? Is this within, say, 25 miles? (Consider travelling time and costs, availability for informal meetings, telephone costs.)

* What maintenance service (e.g. 4-hour response) is he offering and from where?

* What service does he offer in respect of initial system design, user training, planning and change over for initial and subsequent applications and back-up for machine failure?

* Can he name suitable clients to visit? (A check, particularly with actual operating staff, can be very helpful. A telephone call is not really an adequate substitute for a visit.)

The system

* Does the proposed system meet present application requirements and could it be enhanced for the stated future applications?

* How long will it take each day to input the required data? (An estimate is necessary which takes account of time spent on validity queries, etc.)

* How long does it take to copy a disk for back-up purposes?

* How long will it take to print the required reports: daily, weekly and monthly?

* What is the sequence for the installation of the applications and how much time is required for each in respect of file set-up, operator training, parallel running, take-over and bedding down?

* To what extent can the system carry out more than one operation at the same time, viz:
  —Printing for Job 1 while input is proceeding for Job 2?
  —Accepting input for Job 1 from terminal 1 while simultaneously accepting input for Job 2 from terminal 2?
  —Operating as a word processor from terminal 1 while accepting computer work through terminal 2?
  (The first requirement is normally desirable for all but the smallest systems but the others are related only to larger systems.)

* Is there an upward growth path which will not involve changes to the initial programs but will when required allow:
  —Additional floppy disk drives?
  —Addition or change over to hard disks?
  —Additional terminals?
  —Additional main storage?
  (Application areas tend to increase as a user's experience and confidence increase. Work volumes will grow if the volume of business increases.)

* How many user staff will be directly involved? Will they be suitable? What training is needed? And at what cost?

* Have all installation and running costs been taken into account?

Software

The most important aspect of software evaluation is thorough preparation. The requirements statement is essential, for without it there is no yardstick against which to compare the merits of the program being assessed. Although many of the poorer programs can be rejected after a few minutes' evaluation, the search for a professionally prepared program which will make a significant contribution to the efficient running of the business will take time.

With the exception of the first, the following points are not necessarily in order of importance, since that will depend upon individual circumstances.

* Does the program meet requirements? (Check the requirements statement item by item and ensure that all essential features are covered. Obtain written guarantees that the file capacity is adequate for the intended task. Ensure that report layouts are satisfactory.)

* Does the program have good documentation? (The manual is the first source of help for the user. Professionally prepared manuals, intelligible to the layman are essential.)

* Will any of the application packages require modification?

* Can the supplier modify the packages if this is subsequently found desirable?

* Is the program well tried? (All computer programs have faults or 'bugs' when first prepared. The most important faults will be removed during initial testing, but the remainder are normally corrected during use 'in the field'. Programs which have been in extensive use for a reasonable period of time are less likely to contain serious faults.)

* Is the program simple to use? (A well written program will continually guide the user by producing unambiguous prompting messages on the VDU.)

* Does the program have adequate error trapping? (The program should be written such that all keyboard entries are subjected to validity tests. Understandable messages should be produced if

an error occurs. The program should refuse to accept XYZ as an input for an hourly rate.)

* Does the program produce a proper audit trail where necessary?

* Does the supplier offer genuine program maintenance? (The best method of obtaining information on the level of support is to contact existing users.)

* Is adequate training provided and at what cost?

* Is the supplier able to help with program documentation enquiries? (Following introductory training and successful implementation there will be many problems of a relatively minor nature which the supplier should be able to assist with, possibly by means of telephone enquiries. In order to do this the supplier must have a thorough working knowledge of the software.)

* Will program up-dates be supplied and if so, for what charge? (Computer programs are rarely static and in general will be continuously upgraded to take account of experience in the field, or to accommodate changing legislation. It is important to ensure that program up-dates will be made available.)

* Does the program have built-in security and back-up procedures? (If the application requires that certain files should be for restricted access the program must cater for this. In addition, a good software package will include utility routines for the copying of data files and this can speed up the task of obtaining back-up copies.)

* Does the program allow for future integration of separate applications? (See page 40.)

* If printing is temporarily halted, is it necessary to start the print-out from the beginning?

Hardware

Many hardware points are closely linked with software design and these are included in the system checklist.

* Is the hardware manufactured by a sizeable organisation? (This gives some assurance of continuing support.)

* How much disk storage can be on line at one time?

* What is the cost of additional main memory? (Would it be sensible to install more than the supplier suggests in view of the possible lower initial costs compared to the cost of subsequent memory enhancement?

* How fast does the printer operate? How long will it take to print all reports at month end? (Prolonged or excessive printing time is a common criticism.)

* Can the printer supply multiple copies? (Check for clarity.)

* Is the printer a modular unit? (Can it easily be exchanged on failure or up-dating?)

Computing costs

The following items are simply a checklist and not all items will necessarily apply to any one installation.

Initial installation costs

* Computer room/environment: structural changes, power supply, furniture, including safe for disks.

* Hardware costs. The question of buy, lease or rent is partly a financial question – including consideration of capital allowances – and partly a question of expected life for the equipment, bearing in mind its suitability for the business in the future.

* Voltage stabiliser

* Wiring to distant terminals

* Software: utilities and application packages

* Consultancy fees

* Systems analysis and programming provided by supplier

* Staff training, including hotel and travel expenses

* Creating new printed forms: for output and possibly input

* Application conversion: organising and editing data for new files, keying and checking of new files, testing and parallel running. Some of this work may have to be contracted out, or there may be additional overtime to be paid.

Running costs
Salaries for computer input and operating
Hardware maintenance or rental
Computer stationery, ribbons and disks
Finance charges, i.e. loan interest
Insurance

Appendix B

Application Packages

Widely available software packages

General ledger
Incomplete records
Integrated ledger/stock/invoicing
Job costing billing
Mailing system
Payroll
Purchase ledger
Sales ledger
Stock systems
Word processing

Specialised software packages

Appointments systems
Auction system
Cashflow/forecasting
Conference organisation
Database management
Employment agents system
Estate agents system
Factoring systems
Farming/livestock systems
Motor dealers systems

Glossary

This glossary contains explanations of words used in the text and of other words commonly encountered in microcomputing.

The concept of a computer program is so fundamental that it is defined immediately and will subsequently be used as appropriate in the explanations.

Computer program   A list of detailed instructions directing the computer to perform a specific task.

Access time   The length of time between a request for information and its availability.

Address   A number designating a specific storage location in the device.

Algorithm   A set of procedures for solving a problem.

Alphanumeric   A descriptive term for a set of characters consisting of alphabetic, numeric and special characters.

Application program   A set of computer instructions written for a specific user application.

Array   An arrangement of elements (numbers, characters, etc.) in rows and columns.

ASCII   American Standard Code for Information Interchange.

Assembly language   See under **Language**

Backing store   External store of a computer for holding large quantities of data.

BASIC   Beginner's All-purpose Symbolic Instruction Code. A programming language often used with microcomputer systems.

Batch mode   A method of working whereby all data for the application is input to the computer in a continuous stream. When all the data has been input, the program is run and all the data is processed.

Binary A number system with a base of 2. It uses only digits: 0 and 1.

Bit Binary digit. One binary digit is usually represented by '1' or '0' or by 'on' or 'off'.

Buffer storage Any device that temporarily holds data during data transfer, usually between internal and external forms of storage.

Bug A mistake in a *program* causing it to give erroneous results.

Byte A sequence of eight *binary bits* which may be used to represent one character of information.

Central Processing Unit (CPU) This component, commonly known as the microprocessor, performs the tasks of data manipulation and the organisation of peripheral components.

Character A letter, digit, symbol or punctuation mark used to represent one character of information.

COBOL Common Business Oriented Language. A programming language used for data processing in business.

Compiler A *program* that translates, into English-like statements, from a high-level programming language, instructions which the computer can execute immediately.

CP/M Control Program (for) Microcomputers. A commonly used *program* which organises the internal operation of the computer.

Computer program A list of detailed instructions directing the computer to perform a specific task.

Cursor A cursor is an electronically generated symbol (usually a line or a square) appearing on the screen of a video display terminal to indicate where the next character will appear.

Database A pool of shared data with rules which define its structure and how it may be accessed.

Data processing The manipulation of data by the execution of a sequence of instructions. Synonymous with information processing.

Debug To detect, locate and eliminate mistakes in a *program* or a malfunction in a microcomputer's electronic circuits. Similar to the term 'troubleshoot'.

Descenders The tail on some lower case letters.

Diskette   A flexible disk coated with magnetic material used as a data storage medium. Synonymous with the term 'floppy disk'.

Edit   To modify data by inserting, changing or eliminating characters.

Editor   An editor is a *program* that allows a user to edit data or instructions.

Erase   To wipe out information stored in the microcomputer *memory* or in other storage media.

Execute   To carry out the *program* instructions.

Firmware   Computer instructions stored in read only memory.

Floppy disk   See **Diskette**.

FORTRAN   FORmula TRANslator: a high-level computer language used frequently for scientific calculations.

Hardcopy   A printed paper copy of a program or its results produced by a printer attached to a microcomputer.

Hardware   The physical parts of a microcomputer as contrasted with *computer programs (software)*. Compare with *software* and *firmware*.

High-level language   See under **Language**.

Interface   Electronic circuitry specifically designed to link two or more microcomputer devices so as to permit transfer of data between them.

Interpreter   A program that translates each high-level *language program statement* into executable machine instructions each time the high-level statement is encountered during the execution of the user's program. This is a technical function and is of little consequence to the layman.

Language   A set of rules and symbols for passing instructions to a computer.

—*Machine language:* A set of rules or symbols which may be executed immediately by the computer. The symbols will normally be restricted to '0' and '1' and the rules will define the allowed patterns of the symbols.

—*Assembly language:* A language which allows the use of mnemonic symbols instead of patterns of '0' and '1', thereby easing the task of the programmer.

—*High-level language:* A language which allows computer instructions to be written in a restricted form of the English language.

Load   To transfer data from an external data storage device into a microcomputer.

Loop   A sequence of instructions repeated until the loop is terminated.

Machine language   See under *language*.

Memory   Any device used to store data or instructions for the computer. Memory devices are compared in terms of storage capacity, access time and cost.

Menu   A list of options presented to the operator during execution of a *program*.

Microcomputer   A small computer employing a microprocessor as the central processing unit.

Microprocessor   Electronic circuitry on a single integrated circuit chip that can perform data manipulation.

MODEM   Modulation/Demodulation device. It allows computers, terminals and other digital devices to communicate over telephone circuits or other data lines.

Operating system   *A program* which organises the internal operation of the computer. See CP/M.

Peripheral   An external accessory connected to the microcomputer and used for the input-output or storage of data. *Visual display units*, keyboards, line printers. Magnetic storage devices are considered to be peripherals.

Program   A list of computer instruction statements directing the computer to perform specific operations.

Random Access Memory (RAM)   A medium for data or *program* storage, the contents of which may be changed during the operation of the computer. A better name for this type of *memory* would be 'read/write' memory.

Read Only Memory (ROM)   A component of the microcomputer which contains certain instructions required by the computer for its internal use. These instructions cannot be altered by the computer.

Software   Computer *programs* and related documentation usually designed for specific applications and stored on cassette tape, punched paper tape or *floppy disk*. Contrast with *firmware* and *hardware*.

Time-sharing   A system in which *CPU* time and system resources are shared between a number of users, each working on his own.

Turn-key   A complete computer system designed to match the user's requirements exactly.

Visual Display Unit   A terminal with a display screen and (normally) a keyboard.

Volatile memory   *Memory* whose content is lost when electrical power is removed.